FAVORITE

MONTANA RECIPES

WITH BITS OF HISTORY STIRRED IN

Best Wishes from the Big Sky!

Patricia S. Black

Cooked up by

Patricia Scott Black

Illustrated by

William Scott Black

HEART OF THE WEST press

ISBN: 0-9642310-0-X

1st Printing: June 1994
2nd Printing: August 1995
3rd Printing: November 1998
4th Printing: December 2000

Address inquiries:
HEART OF THE WEST PRESS
P.O. Box 80663
Billings, Montana 59102

Typeset by
Melissa Will

Cover Design by
Bill Black and Mike Clark

Published by Heart of the West Press
Printed in Billings, Montana - USA

Ordering information for additional copies
is located at the back of the book.

DEDICATION

This book is dedicated to my loving mom, Emma Christina, who has dedicated so many of her 87 years to me, my brothers, and our families.

and

To my dad, Palmer M. Scott, who touched so many lives with his hope and courage and for the love and encouragement he gave his family.

APPRECIATION

Special appreciation to my husband, Don, who endured my many nights of "burning the midnight oil;" my family, Deb, Bill, Suzie, and Ron; sons-in law, Rick and Dave; daughters-in-law, Colleen and Stacey; grandchildren, Michael, Jonathan, Christina, Kelly Ann and Emma; my brothers, Palmer, Duane, Ron and Ed and their families; my mother, Emma; and my mother-in-law and father-in-law, Bessie and Bill Black. A big thank you to each and everyone for giving me the constant assistance, encouragement, and enthusiasm to complete this cookbook.

TABLE OF CONTENTS

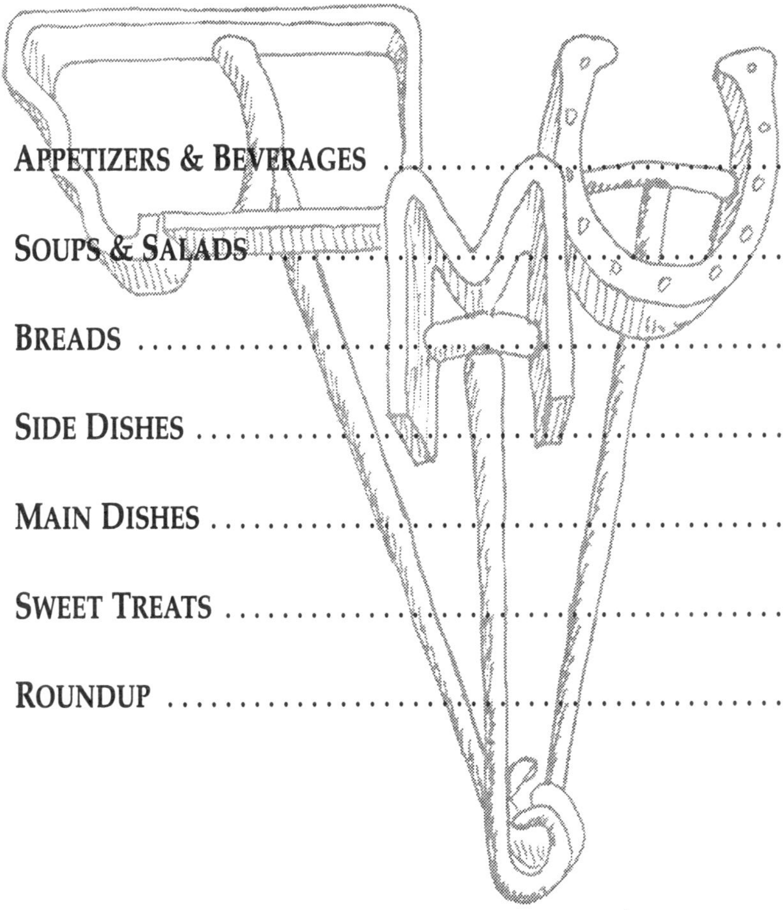

APPETIZERS & BEVERAGES

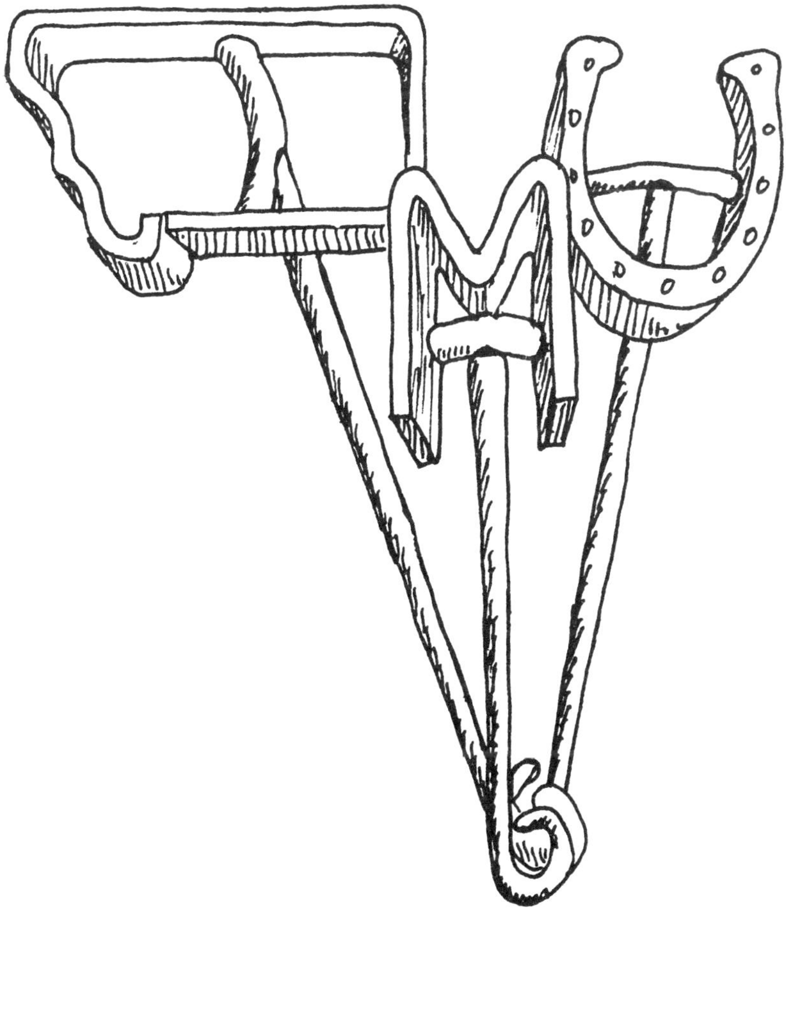

APPETIZERS/BEVERAGES

Montana's State Flower is the Bitterroot. It has soft pink petals and was selected in February of 1895, after the Montana Floral Emblem Association held a statewide vote. The Evening Primrose was the runner-up.

PARTY APPETIZER

1/2 cup chopped onion
1/2 teaspoon garlic powder
1 1/2 cups catsup
1/2 teaspoon salt
2 tablespoons vinegar
1 tablespoon dry mustard
2 tablespoons Worcestershire sauce
1/2 teaspoon pepper
1/2 cup lemon juice
1 cup honey
1 8-ounce package cream cheese

Mix all ingredients except cheese in a saucepan and simmer until onion is tender, about 10-15 minutes. Refrigerate mixture and when ready to serve, pour over cream cheese that has been spread evenly in an 8x8 inch pan. Serve with a basket of crackers of your choosing.

APPETIZERS/BEVERAGES

Ice fishing in Montana is somewhat of a challenge as the cold weather can become a factor. The experts say to dress warm and pack your patience along with your bait, fishing pole, and don't forget an ice auger.

CRAZY MEATBALLS

2 pounds ground beef
1 cup bread crumbs
3 eggs, beaten
1 package onion soup mix
1 16-ounce can sauerkraut
1 can cranberry sauce (whole berry)
1 cup brown sugar
1 bottle chili sauce
1 bottle water (chili sauce bottle)

Mix the first four ingredients and form meatballs about the size of walnuts. Place in baking dish. Combine the rest of the ingredients and pour over meatballs. Bake at 350 degrees for 2 hours. Serves 10-12.

APPETIZERS/BEVERAGES

On September 26, 1910, J.C. "Bud" Mars made the first air flight in Montana at the state fair in Helena. Fair goers were amazed and some could not believe what they had seen. It was the event of the year and was talked about for months.

TACO DIP

Use an 8 inch square pan, add the following ingredients in layers, mixing ingredients for each layer.

First layer:
1 can refried beans

Second layer:
1 1/2 or 2 small avocados, mashed
1 tablespoon lemon juice
1/8 teaspoon pepper
1/4 teaspoon salt

Third layer:
1/2 package taco seasoning
1/2 cup sour cream
1/4 cup mayonnaise

Top with 1/2 cup chopped onions
1 cup chopped tomato
1/2 cup chopped ripe olives
Grated cheese to cover

Serve with tortilla chips or corn chips.

APPETIZERS/BEVERAGES

Shelby was the site of the July 4, 1923, World Heavy Weight championship fight between Jack Dempsey and Tommy Gibbons. The fight began as a publicity event when James W. "Body" Johnson arranged to bring in the world heavy-weight champion, Jack Dempsey, to box Tommy Gibbons. A stadium was built, tickets were printed, and the Great Northern Railway set up more temporary depots in expectation of thousands of fans coming to town for the match. At the last minute, Dempsey's manager reneged but later reconsidered and fulfilled the contract, but it was too late as trains had been canceled and people lost interest. Dempsey won the 15 round fight by decision; but promoters lost over $100,000.

SHRIMP DIP

1 8-ounce package cream cheese
1 can shrimp, drained
3 tablespoons chili sauce
1/2 teaspoon Worcestershire sauce
2 teaspoons scraped onion juice and pulp
1 teaspoon lemon juice
1 tablespoon mayonnaise

Combine all ingredients and beat until creamy. Serve with potato chips.

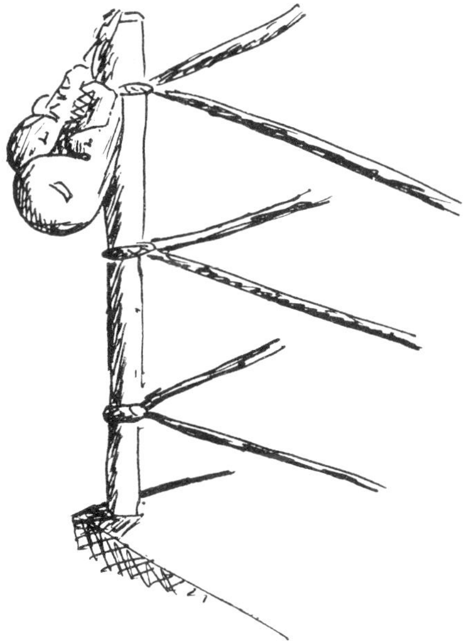

APPETIZERS/BEVERAGES

The first telephones in Montana began ringing in Butte on February 21, 1882, when sixteen businesses and homes were connected. Soon other cities were operating telephone exchanges and telephone companies began to expand. The operators became a part of the family.

HOT CHEESE DIP

1/2 pound Velvetta cheese, melted
3/4 cup mayonnaise
1/2 cup sour cream
10 green onions, chopped
Cayenne pepper, a shake or two
1 teaspoon Worcestershire sauce
1 can crab or shrimp (6-ounce size)

Mix ingredients together and serve with any type of chips or vegetables.

CREAMY DILL DIP

1/2 cup mayonnaise
1/2 cup sour cream
2 teaspoons dill weed
1 teaspoon sugar
1 teaspoon dry onion
1/4 teaspoon salt
1/4 teaspoon pepper

Mix ingredients together and chill several hours. Good with chicken sticks.

PINEAPPLE CHEESE BALL

2 8-ounce packages cream cheese, softened
1 can crushed pineapple, drained
2 cups chopped pecans
1/4 cup finely chopped green pepper
2 tablespoons finely chopped onion
1 1/2 teaspoons seasoned salt

Beat cheese until smooth. Gradually stir in crushed pineapple, 1 cup pecans, green peppers, onion, and salt. Shape into ball. Roll in remaining pecans. Wrap in plastic or foil. Refrigerate until well chilled. Serve on tray surrounded with crackers or sliced party bread.

The Western Meadowlark was declared the State Bird by the Legislature in March of 1931, following a referendum vote of Montana school children.

WILD WEST CHILI DIP

1 pound hamburger, browned and drained
2 pounds processed cheese (Velvetta)
2 cans chili, without beans
Dash of chili powder (optional)

Melt cheese in crock pot on low temperature. Add browned hamburger and chili. Stir well. Keep pot on warm. Serve with tortilla chips as dippers.

The Berkeley Pit located in Butte was begun in 1955. It was the largest truck operated open pit copper mine in the United States. The Pit is 7,000 feet in length, 5,600 feet in width and is more than 1,800 feet in depth. The underground mines were gradually phased out and all copper mining ceased in 1982.

WHAT-NOTS

Filling:
1 pound hamburger
2 teaspoons salt
1/4 teaspoon pepper
1 small onion, chopped fine
1/2 teaspoon cayenne pepper
1/4 teaspoon garlic
1/2 can tomato paste
1/2 teaspoon chili powder

Mix above ingredients together.

Pastry:
3/4 cup butter
1 1/2 cups cottage cheese
2 1/2 cups flour
1/3 cup cold water

Mix and roll out. Cut small circles. Place small amount of filling on each circle. Fold over or pull to top and pinch together. Place on cookie sheet and bake at 425 degrees for 20 minutes or a bit longer.

APPETIZERS/BEVERAGES

Montana is home to several North American Indian Tribes: the Assiniboine-Sioux, Blackfeet, Chippewa-Cree, Confederate Salish and Kootenai, Crow, Assiniboine-Gros Ventre, and the Northern Cheyenne.

MEATBALL APPETIZERS

1 pound ground round
1 egg
1 tablespoon cream
Salt and pepper
2-3 tablespoons flour
2 tablespoons butter
1 cup chili sauce
1/2 cup grape jelly

Combine meat, salt, pepper, egg and cream. Add just enough flour to hold mixture together. Form about 60 miniature meatballs and brown them in the butter. Beat chili sauce and grape jelly together until smooth. Add sauce to browned, drained meatballs, cover and simmer about 30 minutes. Serve warm.

The Festival of Nations held in Red Lodge every summer since August 5, 1950, is a spectacular event lasting nine days. Descendants of Scandinavians, Scots, Italians, Slavs, Germans and other ethnic groups hold on to their traditions as they don their native costumes, dance the country folk dances, prepare native foods, eat, and enjoy the colorful summer festival that thousands of visitors and residents attend each year.

BRAUNSCHWEIGER PATE

1 pound Braunschweiger, broken up
1 8-ounce package cream cheese, softened
1 tablespoon milk
1 tablespoon grated onion
1 teaspoon sugar
1 scant teaspoon chili powder

Combine the above ingredients using only half of the cream cheese and beat until smooth. Form igloo shape (small bowl), cover and chill. Whip remaining cream cheese, **1 tablespoon milk**, and **1/8 teaspoon bottled hot pepper sauce** until smooth, adding a **dash of salt**, if you prefer. Unmold first mixture and cover with cream cheese mixture. Garnish with parsley and serve with your favorite crackers.

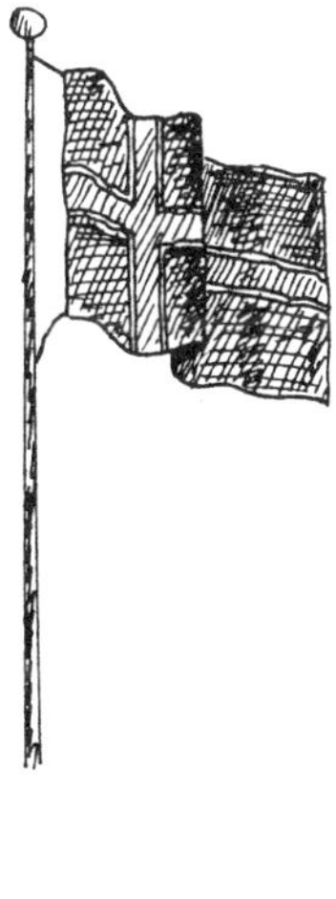

MONTANA APRICOT SLUSH

1 pint apricot brandy
1 cup vodka
1 46-ounce can pineapple juice
1 46-ounce can apricot nectar
1 12-ounce can frozen orange juice
1 12-ounce can frozen lemonade

Combine above ingredients and freeze. When ready to serve, fill glass 1/2 to 3/4 full of frozen slush then fill remainder of glass with **7-Up**.

CHAP SNAPPER

1 shot Bailey's Irish Creme
1 shot butterscotch schnapps

Pour over ice to cool, then into liqueur glass.

HUMMERS

1/4 cup creme de mint
1/4 cup creme de cacao
4 cups chocolate ice cream

Mix above ingredients together and serve over crushed ice.

Everyone dreams of a warm cabin on a winter's night with snow falling gently and a glowing fire in the stove. In Montana, those dreams come true. Montana is truly a winter wonderland.

HOT BUTTERED RUM
"a nice warm drink"

4 sticks butter (do not substitute)
1 (16-ounce) box light brown sugar
2 teaspoons ground cinnamon
1 teaspoon ground nutmeg
1 quart vanilla ice cream, softened
Light rum

Combine butter, sugar, cinnamon, and nutmeg; beating until light and fluffy. Add ice cream; stir until well blended. Spoon into container and freeze. To serve, thaw slightly and place 3 tablespoons of the mixture and 1 ounce of rum in a large mug and fill with boiling water. Stir well. Top with whipped cream, if you wish. (Unused butter mixture may be refrozen.)

Taking in a rodeo under the Big Sky will bring cause for excitement as the horses buck a little harder and the bulls are a little meaner. The Wolf Point Stampede comes to mind as it has the honor of being the oldest, professional rodeo in the state.

COW PUNCHER

3 ounces bourbon
1 ounce brandy (not fruit flavored)
3 tablespoons sugar
1 teaspoon vanilla
2 cups milk
6 to 8 ice cubes

Blend all ingredients in a blender until frothy; serve immediately.

FESTIVE PUNCH

1 large can pineapple juice
2 large cans apricot-orange juice
1 quart apple juice
2 quarts ginger ale
1 quart orange sherbet

Combine fruit juices and ginger ale in punch bowl. Float sherbet in punch. Serves 45-50.

"Ski Montana" is a bumper sticker seen throughout the USA. Skiing is a way of life in Montana, boasting 15 resorts. After a long day on the slopes, a hot drink and an inviting fire, some skiing enthusiasts say, "It doesn't get any better than this."

HOLIDAY HOT SPICED WINE

"heartwarming"

2 cups sugar
10 whole cloves
8 cinnamon sticks
4 cups water
3 lemons, thinly sliced
1/2 cup brandy
1/2 gallon red wine

In a 5-quart kettle, combine sugar, cloves, cinnamon sticks, and water; bring to a boil, stirring constantly. Boil uncovered 5 minutes and remove from heat, adding sliced lemons. Let stand, covered, 10 minutes. With a slotted spoon, lift out cloves and cinnamon sticks. Add brandy and wine; simmer until hot. Serve in mugs. This can be covered and stored in the refrigerator.

STRAWBERRY SPRITZER

1 10-ounce package sliced, sweetened, frozen strawberries
4 ounces light rum
2 tablespoons lemon juice
1 12-ounce bottle club soda, chilled

Thaw strawberries just until they can be separated. Whirl in a blender with rum and lemon juice until berries are pureed. Divide among four glasses. Add soda and stir. Serve at once.

HOT SPICED CIDER

2 quarts apple cider
1/2 cup brown sugar
1/4 teaspoon salt
2 sticks cinnamon
1 teaspoon whole cloves

Heat all ingredients in a saucepan to boiling point. Reduce heat and simmer 10 minutes. Remove spices and serve.

SOUPS & SALADS

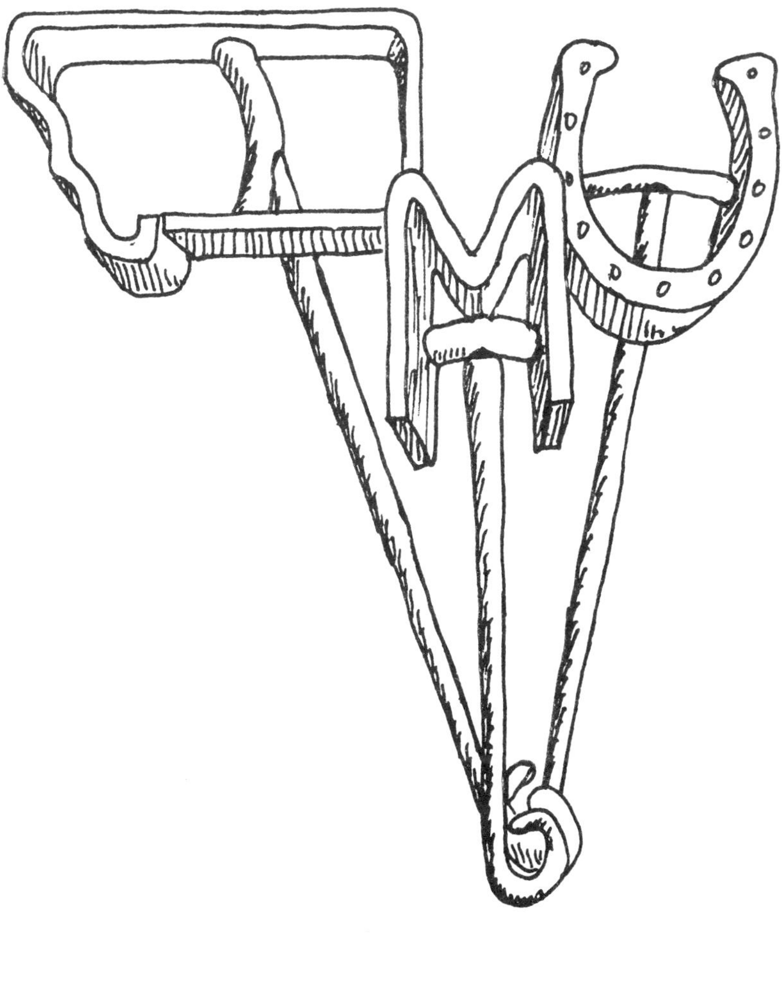

ED'S MOM'S VEGETABLE SOUP

1 pound beef stew meat or soup meat
1 large can tomatoes
3 stalks celery, chopped
2 medium potatoes, cubed
1 large onion, chopped
2 medium-large carrots, cubed
1 package frozen okra, sliced
1 package frozen corn
1 package frozen green beans, chopped

Water to cover and cook until vegetables are tender. The key ingredient is okra which can be found in most large markets' frozen food section. This soup goes good with corn bread.

MRS. BAKER'S SPINACH SOUP

"an old German recipe"

1 bunch of spinach
Tops of 2 green onions
1 big sprig of green dill
2 or 3 medium potatoes
2 tablespoons sour cream
Salt
Vinegar

Wash spinach well, add onions (chopped) and dill. Put in large kettle and cover with water and boil until done. Add salt to taste. Boil 2 or 3 potatoes separately, then dice. Add to spinach mixture. Add sour cream, then vinegar to taste.

Montana has a wealth of rich natural resources. It supplies the nation and the world with water, timber, coal, silver and gold, oil, copper, and natural gas. A "Treasure State" it is.

BEST EVER CLAM CHOWDER SOUP

- 1 1/2 cups finely chopped onion
- 1 1/2 cups finely chopped celery
- 3 cups finely chopped potatoes
- 1 1/8 cups butter (no substitute)
- 3 cans minced clams
- 1 1/8 cups flour
- 1 1/2 quarts half and half
- 2 tablespoons salt
- 3 tablespoons apple cider vinegar
- 2 chicken bouillon cubes

Combine all vegetables and salt, simmering in drained clam juice until tender. Melt butter in large heavy pan, add flour and stir until smooth. Stir in half and half and cook slowly until thickened. Stir constantly. Add vegetables, clams, bouillon cubes and simmer on very low heat as it scorches easily.

In some parts of Montana, the growing season is quite short and many gardeners begin planting as early as the Farmer's Almanac allows. The growing seasons vary in length from 80 frost-free days in some mountain valleys to 141 days in the eastern plains counties. The average annual rainfall is 15 inches while the average daytime temperatures vary from 28 degrees in January to 84 degrees in July.

CREAM OF TOMATO SOUP

2 cups canned or fresh chopped tomatoes
1/2 cup chopped celery
1/4 cup each of chopped onion and carrots
1 teaspoon sugar
1/2 teaspoon basil
Pinch of marjoram and bay leaves
1 tablespoon margarine
1/2 cup chicken stock
1 tablespoon chicken bouillon granules or 1 cube
2 tablespoons butter or margarine
2 tablespoons flour
2 cups half and half
1/4 cup sour cream
Dash of paprika and dash of pepper

Simmer all vegetables, sugar, herbs, and 1 tablespoon margarine in stock until soft. Then melt 2 tablespoons margarine in small saucepan; add flour and cook 3 minutes. Combine this mixture with half and half, paprika and pepper with vegetables. Simmer 20 minutes. Blend in sour cream. DO NOT BOIL. Garnish with chopped tomatoes or dollops of mayonnaise seasoned with curry powder or parsley. Serve hot or cold.

Even before statehood, Montana women had tried to gain the power to vote. After several attempts, suffrage was finally achieved on November 3, 1914.

MONTANA BEAN SOUP

Wash **3 cups of assorted beans** thoroughly and place in large kettle. Cover with water and add **2 tablespoons salt.** Soak overnight. In the morning, drain and add **2 quarts water** along with **ham hocks or ham.** Bring to boil, then simmer slowly for at least 2 1/2 to 3 hours.

Add:
1 large chopped onion
1 quart stewed tomatoes
1 teaspoon chili powder (scant)
Juice of 1 lemon or 3 tablespoons bottled lemon juice
Suspicion of garlic powder

Simmer at least 1 hour. Serve with crackers. For variation, thinly sliced carrots may be added to the beans.

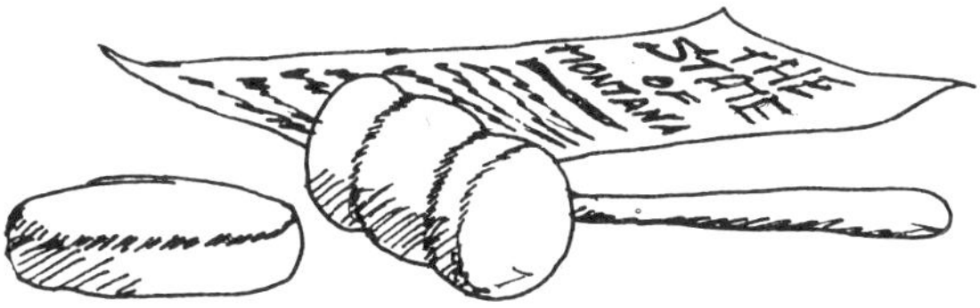

Forest lands cover almost one fourth of Montana's area. Some of the major commercial trees include the Douglas Fir, Ponderosa Pine, western white pine larch, and the lodgepole pine. The Ponderosa Pine is the State Tree, chosen in 1949.

TOMATO SOUP SALAD

1 can condensed tomato soup
2 packages unflavored gelatin
1/2 cup water
1 can tuna or crab or shrimp (6-ounce size)
1 carton cottage cheese or cream cheese (8-ounce size) ***(If using cream cheese, add it to soup mixture while hot and beat with beater until smooth).***
1 cup diced celery
1 cup mayonnaise
Salt and pepper to taste
2 hard boiled eggs, chopped

Bring soup to boil without any liquid added. Dissolve gelatin in water and add to soup mixture. Let cool. Add tuna, celery, cottage cheese, mayonnaise, salt and pepper, and eggs to cooled soup mixture. Set to congeal. An extra can of shrimp and/or crab can be also added. Serves 8.

Two of the largest rivers in the United States, the Missouri and Columbia, rise in Montana. The Missouri River joins the Mississippi, which drains into the Gulf of Mexico. The Columbia drains into the Pacific Ocean. The St. Mary's and Belly Rivers drain into the Hudson Bay. Montana is the only state that can boast of rivers draining into the Pacific Ocean, Gulf of Mexico, and Hudson Bay.

SAUERKRAUT SALAD

Combine:
1 can sauerkraut, drained and rinsed
1 cup chopped celery
1/2 cup chopped green pepper
1/4 cup chopped onion
1/4 cup chopped canned pimentos

Boil together:
1/4 cup sugar
1/4 cup vinegar
1/2 cup water

Add to sauerkraut mixture and let stand overnight.

Winters in Montana can be very cold and summers can be very hot. The coldest temperature recorded was 70 degrees below zero on January 20, 1954 on Rogers Pass near Lincoln. The hottest temperature of 117 degrees was recorded in Glendive in August of 1893 and in Medicine Lake in July of 1937.

CHICKEN SALAD I

4 chicken breasts, cooked, cut in bite size pieces
1 can water chestnuts, sliced thin
1 cup grapes, cut in half
1/2 cup salad dressing
1/4 cup lemon juice
1/2 teaspoon curry powder
1/2 teaspoon salt
1 package toasted slivered almonds

Combine all ingredients. Chill four hours, serve on lettuce. Garnish with whole grapes and almonds.

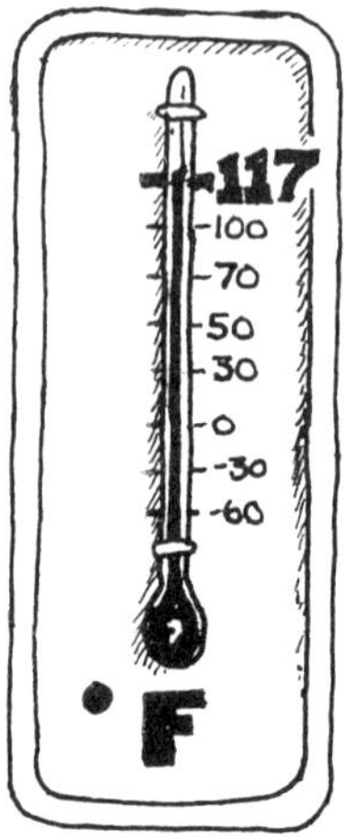

John Colter, a member of the Lewis and Clark Exhibition, was the first white man to come up on "Colter's Hell" or Yellowstone Park as it has been officially named. When Colter returned to St. Louis, he told his friends of the geysers and the boiling pools and his run for life with the Blackfeet Indians not far behind. John Colter was a heroic mountain man.

CHICKEN SALAD II

3 cups diced chicken
2 cups pineapple chunks
1 cup chopped walnuts
1 cup chopped celery
2 cups sour cream
1 1/3 cups mayonnaise
1 cup grated cheese

Mix mayonnaise and sour cream. Stir in rest of ingredients and save enough cheese to sprinkle a little on top of salad. Place in a 9x13 inch pan. Serve on a lettuce leaf.

Hutterite Colonies are located throughout Montana with about 4,000 members living in 41 colonies. They are Anabaptists and practice community of goods. The Hutterites are excellent farmers and frequently have vegetables and poultry for sale.

TASTY FRESH SALAD

2 heads of broccoli
1 head cauliflower
1 can black olives
1 can water chestnuts
1 package Italian dressing mix
1 bottle Italian dressing (small bottle, using one half)

Slice tops of broccoli, break cauliflower into florets and slice into bite sized pieces. Slice olives and water chestnuts. Sprinkle dry mix on vegetables and add 1/2 of the bottled dressing. Make ahead so salad has a chance to marinate.

If you listen on a quiet summer night, you can hear the coyotes howling at the moon. It has been noted that there is power in numbers as coyotes sometimes travel in packs and usually can drive off a grizzly bear or a mountain lion. The coyote is an adaptable animal and is seen throughout the state.

SHRIMP AND CRAB SALAD

"an elegant dish"

1 large loaf of white bread
1 medium minced onion (less if you choose)
5 boiled eggs, chopped

Trim crusts off bread, butter each slice; cube (16 cubes per slice). Mix bread cubes, onion, and eggs. Refrigerate overnight. A 9x13 inch covered container is helpful.

In the morning, add:
2 cans shrimp
1 cup crab
1 cup chopped celery
1 1/2 to 2 cups mayonnaise
1 teaspoon dry mustard
1 teaspoon celery salt

Mix and refrigerate at least 4 hours before serving.

Winters can get long for many a Montanan and in the evenings a lot of card playing goes on. Whist is a popular card game and if you think you are ready for the big time, Glasgow holds a whist tournament every November. With skill, a bit of a Scandinavian accent, and some luck, Montanans and friends across the border gather for some high stakes.

JUDI'S SHRIMP SALAD

Mix and chill:
3 cans shrimp (washed)
1 large can (8 1/2 ounces) sliced water chestnuts
1 can (303) bean sprouts, drained
1 1/2 cups celery (chopped)
1/2 medium onion (chopped)

Toss just before serving, with **two 3-ounce cans Chinese noodles** and dressing.

Dressing:
1 cup mayonnaise
2 tablespoons lemon juice
1/4 teaspoon ginger

Montana is proud of its educational facilities. Located throughout the state are six colleges/universities, five vocational technical centers, three community colleges, seven tribal colleges and three private colleges.

LAYERED DELIGHT SALAD

- **1 head lettuce**
- **Several stalks of celery, chopped fine**
- **1 sliced onion**
- **1 can water chestnuts, sliced thin**
- **1 10-ounce package frozen peas**
- **2 cups mayonnaise**
- **2 tablespoons sugar**
- **8 hard cooked eggs**
- **8 slices bacon, crisply cooked and crumpled**

Tear lettuce in small pieces into a large salad bowl or 9x13 inch glass pan. Add in layers of celery, water chestnuts, onion, and peas. Cover with mayonnaise; sprinkle sugar evenly over mayonnaise. Top with sliced eggs and bacon. Cover with plastic wrap. Refrigerate 8 hours before serving. Serves 12.

Former Governor Stan Stephens submitted the following recipe, mentioning this is a salad that he and former first lady, Ann Stephens, enjoy. Governor Stephens held the state's highest office from 1988 to 1992, choosing not to seek a second term.

PRETZEL STRAWBERRY SALAD

2 1/2 cups coarsely crushed pretzels
3 tablespoons powdered sugar
3/4 cup melted butter
1 8-ounce package cream cheese, softened
1 egg
1 cup powdered sugar
1 9-ounce whipped topping
1 6-ounce strawberry gelatin
2 cups boiling water
2 10-ounce packages frozen strawberries

Mix pretzels, 3 tablespoons powdered sugar, and melted butter. Press into 9x13 inch pan and bake at 350 degrees for 10 minutes. Cool. Beat cream cheese, egg, and 1 cup powdered sugar, then add whipped topping. Spread on pretzels and refrigerate. Mix gelatin and boiling water. Add frozen strawberries. Let thicken and spread on top. Refrigerate 4 hours before serving.

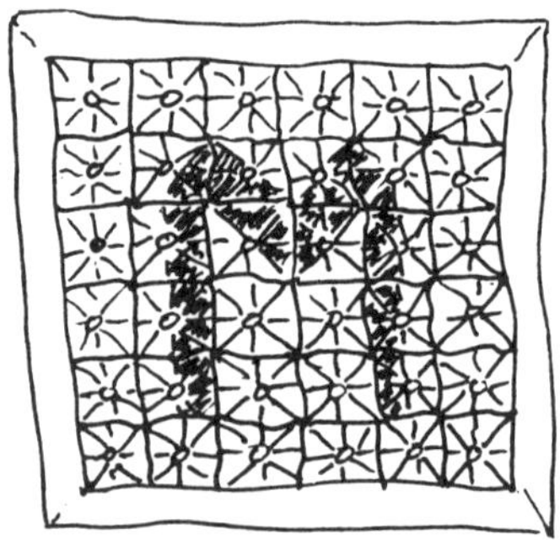

Homegrown food was probably introduced into Montana in 1842 by the Catholic Missionaries in the Bitterroot Valley when they brought in cattle for herds and seeds for planting - the first farming and ranching in Montana.

MOLDED ALMOND FRUIT SALAD

1 3-ounce package lemon gelatin
1 cup boiling water
1 8-ounce package cream cheese
2 cups drained pineapple tidbits
1 package sliced almonds (2 3/4 ounces)
1 cup maraschino cherries (sliced or chopped)
1 cup whipping cream

Put first three ingredients in blender and blend until velvet-like texture forms. Chill until it begins to set. Drain pineapple and maraschino cherries. Whip cream (non-dairy whipped topping may be substituted, but cream is best). When gelatin mixture is set enough to mound on a spoon, fold in fruit and nuts. Fold cream in last. Pour into 8x8 inch square pan or mold. Recipe can be doubled for 9x13 inch pan.

Montanans realize the importance of preserving the state's history. In many communities, museums have long been a part of this endeavor. To add to the preservation of the state, the Montana Historical Society, Western Heritage Center, Museum of the Northern Plains, and the Museum of the Rockies welcome anyone to share the well kept history of Montana.

RASPBERRY SALAD

2 packages (3 ounce size) raspberry gelatin
2 cups boiling water
2 cups frozen raspberries
1/2 cup applesauce
Whipped cream or topping

Dissolve gelatin in the boiling water, stirring well. Add frozen raspberries to the hot mixture. Add applesauce. Mix well and pour into 8x8 inch pan and let set. Top with whipped cream.

The Centennial Ball held at the State Capitol in Helena on November 8, 1989, brought nearly 5,000 Montanans to the city to raise a toast to the State's first one hundred years of statehood. Dancing to the sounds of seven bands playing throughout the Legislative Chambers and meeting rooms was a gala affair for all who attended.

CRANBERRY HOLIDAY SALAD

1 6-ounce package raspberry gelatin
1 cup boiling water
1 16-ounce can whole cranberry sauce
1 13-ounce can undrained crushed pineapple
1 8-ounce package cream cheese
1 pint sour cream
2/3 cup apple juice
1 cup chopped nuts

Dissolve gelatin in boiling water. Add pineapple and cranberry sauce. Add apple juice and nuts. Pour half of mixture into square pan. Chill until firm. Cream together cream cheese and sour cream. Spread over chilled firm gelatin. Put back into refrigerator to chill. Add remaining gelatin over top, chill. Use a 9x13 inch pan if doubling the recipe.

Snowmobiling in Montana usually begins in late November and ends in March. With nearly 3,000 miles of trails you can see some of the most spectacular scenery in the world, get a glimpse of wildlife, and enjoy a touch of nature.

CRANBERRY SALAD MOLD

"a festive salad"

2 cups fresh or canned cranberries
1 cup sugar
1 cup water
Few drops of lemon juice
1 small package of raspberry or strawberry gelatin
15 large marshmallows
1 cup chopped nuts
1 cup chopped celery
1 cup grated peeled apples

Combine cranberries, sugar, water, and lemon juice in large saucepan; cook until cranberries pop. Stir in gelatin and marshmallows until gelatin is dissolved; remove from heat. Cool. Stir in remaining ingredients. Pour into a large mold or 8 small molds. Chill until firm.

BREADS

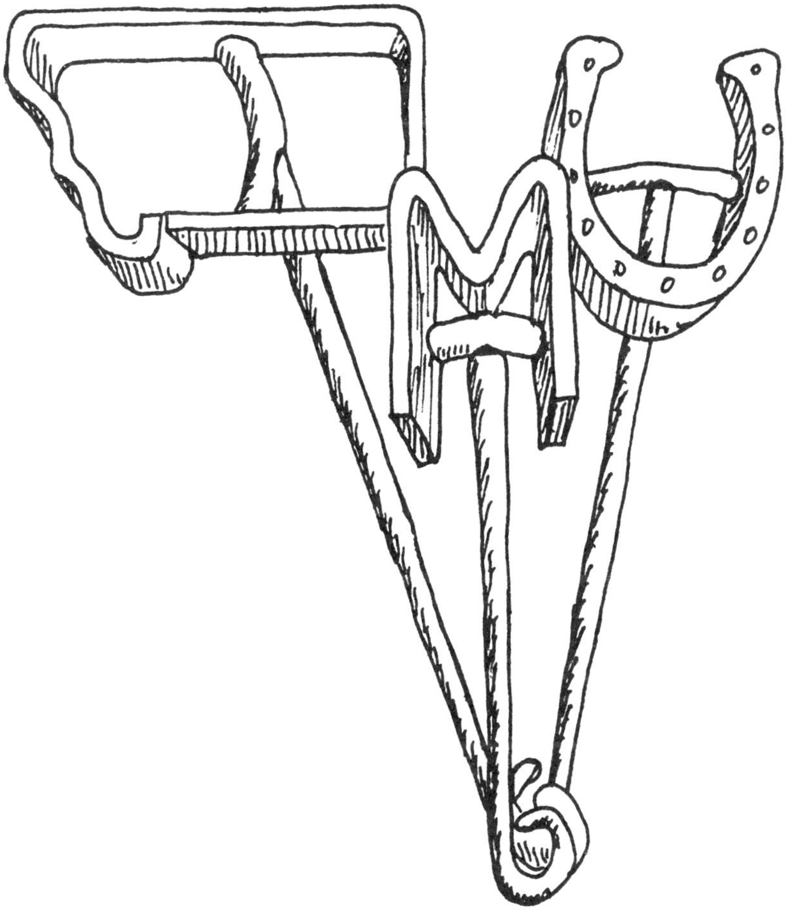

SWEDISH RYE BREAD

"especially good for open-faced sandwiches"

2 cups rye flour (sifted)
1 cup milk (scalded)
3 cups warm water
3/4 cup brown sugar
1/2 cup shortening (melted)
2 packages dry yeast
1/2 cup dark molasses
1 teaspoon anise seed (put in milk)
2 teaspoons salt
5 cups white flour

Dissolve yeast in 1/2 cup warm water, add remaining water and scalded milk. Add salt, sugar, shortening and molasses. Mix rye flour into this mixture with a spoon. Mix flour until easy to handle, then add approximately 5 more cups white flour and knead well. Form into ball in greased bowl, let rise until double. Punch down and let rise again. Make into loaves, let rise about 1 hour. Bake 50-60 minutes at 325-350 degrees. (2 loaves)

BREADS

Willard E. Fraser, the late mayor, was a vibrant, spirited man. He served the city of Billings in the late sixties and early seventies. The bread recipe below was featured in the Billings Gazette while he was still in office. He considered it his favorite recipe, saying "that homemade bread is the most exotic food and rarest of today's epicurean delights."

MAYOR FRASER'S BREAD

1 package yeast
2 tablespoons shortening
3 tablespoons sugar
1 tablespoon salt
7 cups of flour, more or less

Dissolve yeast in **1/2 cup warm water,** let set about 10 minutes. Pour **2 cups hot water** over shortening, sugar, and salt in large bowl. Mix. Add part of flour, mix well. Add yeast mixture. Add remaining flour and knead well until enough flour is absorbed and does not cling to bread board. Place in greased bowl and give half turn. Cover and place in barely warm oven until twice its bulk. Punch down, turn and let rise again till just about twice its size. Form in 2 loaves and let rise again (about 45-60 minutes). Bake in hot oven (400 degrees) for 35 minutes. You may wish to give the tops of the loaves a swish of butter when taken from the oven.

BREADS

Many Montana farm families grind their own flour. They say this makes for tastier and lighter rolls and other baked goods. Coffee pots are on early in the morning in the Big Sky. A fresh roll and a cup of java is a good way to begin the day.

BUTTER HORN ROLLS

6 eggs, beaten
2 1/2 cups very warm milk
1 cup shortening (part butter) melted in hot milk
6 1/2 cups whole wheat flour
2 cups white flour (may not need exactly 2 cups)
2 teaspoons salt
1/2 cup brown sugar or honey
2 packages yeast (2 tablespoons) dissolved in 1/4 cup very warm water with 1 teaspoon sugar. Mix until dissolved and starts to rise.

Mix all together and place in greased bowl, turning once to grease surface; cover and let rise twice before shaping into rolls. Bake at 375 degrees for about 12 to 15 minutes.

Wheat germ could be sprinkled over rolls before baking. The above roll recipe can also be used for cinnamon rolls.

Raising sheep in Montana is still a very productive business. The first sizeable herd arrived in the state in 1865. Other sheep ranches were soon established and today Montana is the fourth largest sheep producing state.

ORANGE ROLLS

1 cup scalded milk
3 tablespoons butter
1/2 cup sugar
1/2 teaspoon salt
1 package dry yeast
3 eggs, beaten
4 cups flour

Creamed Mixture:
1/2 cup melted butter
1/2 cup sugar
Grated rind of orange

Melt butter in scalded milk. When lukewarm, add yeast. Combine yeast mixture, beaten eggs, and sugar. Add 2 cups flour, beat well but do not knead. Let rise 2 hours. Add 2 more cups of flour and let rise 2 more hours. Roll on floured board as for cinnamon rolls. Spread with creamed mixture. Roll up and cut into 30 pieces. Put in oiled muffin tins and let rise 2 hours. Bake at 400 degrees for 8-10 minutes. Serve warm.

Montana is bordered on the east by North Dakota and South Dakota, on the west by Idaho, and on the south by Wyoming and a short section of Idaho. The Canadian provinces of British Columbia, Alberta, and Saskatchewan are our northern neighbors and provide frequent visitors to our state.

CARROT-HONEY DATE MUFFINS

1/4 cup butter
1/2 cup honey
1/2 cup milk
2 large eggs
1 tablespoon grated orange rind
2 cups flour
1 tablespoon baking powder
1 teaspoon salt
1 cup diced pitted dates
1 cup grated carrots

Melt butter with honey. Remove from heat. Stir in milk, eggs, and orange rind. Beat to blend and set aside. Combine dry ingredients and stir thoroughly. Stir in butter mixture and then carrots and dates. Spoon in greased muffin tins and bake at 425 degrees for 15-20 minutes. Test with toothpick for doneness. Let stand for 5 minutes before removing from tins.

To celebrate Montana's 100 years of statehood, a group of Montana residents organized a Montana Centennial Cattle Drive. The Drive began on Labor Day, 1989 in Roundup and headed for Billings, lasting six days. Over 3,000 cowboys and cowgirls herded more that 2,800 cattle through sixty miles of challenge and excitement to make it the success it was and to commemorate the livestock business which is one of Montana's greater industries.

CHEESE AND BACON CORN MUFFINS

"serve with chili on a winter's night"

8 strips bacon, diced
1 cup chopped onions
1 1/4 cups flour
3/4 cup yellow cornmeal
1/3 cup sugar
3 1/2 teaspoons baking powder
1 teaspoon salt
2 eggs
1 cup milk
3 tablespoons melted butter
1 1/4 cups (5 ounces) sharp shredded Cheddar cheese

In a 10 to 12 inch frying pan, stir bacon over medium heat until crisp. Lift out bacon with slotted spoon. Discard all but two tablespoons fat. Add onion. Cook and stir until limp. In a bowl; mix flour, cornmeal, sugar, baking powder, and salt. Beat eggs and milk with butter; stir into flour mixture just until moistened. Mix in bacon, onions, and 3/4 cup cheese. Fill greased large (2 3/4 to 3 inch size) muffin cups two-thirds full with batter. Sprinkle with remaining cheese. Bake in 400 degree oven until a wooden pick inserted in center of muffin comes out clean, about 20 minutes. Remove from pans, cool on racks and serve warm. Makes about 16-18.

Great Falls, Montana's second largest city, was named for the nearby falls of the Missouri River of which Lewis and Clark came upon on June 13, 1805. Charles Marion Russell made his home in Great Falls from 1897 until his death in 1926. The C.M. Russell Auction is held each year in the Electric City to honor this famous artist.

BREAKFAST MUFFINS

"so good and so good for you"

6 cups bran buds
2 cups boiling water
(pour over bran buds)
1 cup shortening
4 eggs
2 1/2 cups sugar
5 cups flour
1 1/2 teaspoons salt
2 tablespoons baking soda
1 quart buttermilk

Cream sugar and shortening. Add one egg at a time. Cream well. Combine flour, soda, and salt. Mix with the creamed mixture, a little at a time, adding a little buttermilk until all is used, then add bran buds. You may add nuts or raisins if desired. Store mixture in refrigerator in covered bowl, using only as much as needed. This batter keeps well for several weeks. Bake in greased muffin tins for 20 minutes at 400 degrees.

A Sweet Pea Carnival, first held in Bozeman in 1906, has since been revived in that city. Sweet Peas grew lavishly in the area at that time and two hundred entries were lined up for the first parade. Bozeman brought back the Festival in 1978. There is entertainment for the whole family at this three-day festivity including the entering and judging of the fragrant Sweet Pea flower.

BLUEBERRY MUFFINS

1 egg
1/2 cup milk
1/4 cup vegetable oil
1 1/2 cups flour
1/2 cup sugar
2 teaspoons baking powder
1/2 teaspoon salt
1 1/2 cups fresh blueberries or one 17-ounce can berries, drained

Grease muffin pans or paper cups set in muffin pan. Beat egg with fork in a mixing bowl and stir in milk and oil. In smaller bowl, blend flour, sugar, baking powder and salt. Stir into egg mixture. Mix until flour is moistened, leaving batter lumpy. Fold in blueberries. Fill muffin cups two-thirds full. Bake 20-25 minutes in 400 degree oven. Serve warm with butter. Yield 12.

Montana's National Guard First Regiment of Infantry was organized in 1887. The Guard's Companies were located in various towns throughout Montana.

BANANA BREAD

1 1/4 cups sugar
1/2 cup shortening
2 eggs
2 1/2 tablespoons sour cream
2 1/2 cups flour
1 teaspoon baking soda
1 teaspoon baking powder
1/2 teaspoon salt
3 or 4 very ripe bananas, mashed
1/2 cup chopped nuts

Cream sugar and shortening together; add eggs, one at a time, beating after each. Add sour cream. Sift dry ingredients together and add to egg mixture alternating with the bananas. Fold in nuts. Bake in 2 greased loaf pans at 325 degrees for about 45-55 minutes, using the toothpick test. Let rest in pans for 15 minutes before removing. The secret to good banana bread is using very ripe bananas.

BREADS

Orchards in the Flathead Valley are popular spots in July and August. Located in western Montana, the famous Flathead Cherries are ripe for picking and eating at that time or if you would rather, you can stop at one of the many fruitstands along the Flathead Lake.

ZUCCHINI BREAD

3 eggs, beaten
1 cup oil
1 cup brown sugar
1 cup white sugar
3 tablespoons vanilla
2 cups ground zucchini
2 1/2 cups flour
1/2 teaspoon baking soda
1/2 teaspoon baking powder
2 teaspoons salt
1 cup coarsely chopped walnuts

Beat eggs, oil, sugars, and flavoring. Add ground zucchini. Slowly add flour, soda, baking powder, and salt. Stir in walnuts. Pour batter into two prepared 9x5x3 inch loaf pans and bake at 350 degrees for 40 minutes, using the toothpick test.

BREADS

In 1850, John Owen purchased St. Mary's Mission, located in the Bitterroot Valley, for $250.00. He and his wife, Nancy, set up fur trading and renamed the mission, Fort Owen. John Owen was a friendly sort and the Fort was the center for many a holiday celebration. The sale of this property was the first recorded in the present Montana.

CHRISTMAS BREAD

2 cups scalded milk
1 tablespoon sugar
2 teaspoons salt
2 packages yeast
1/4 cup warm water
3 cups flour

Cream together:
1/2 cup shortening
3/4 cup sugar
2 teaspoons grated lemon peel (optional)
1 teaspoon vanilla
1/4 teaspoon nutmeg
2 eggs, beaten
Flour
1/2 package fruit mix
2 cups seeded raisins

Soften yeast in the warm water. Add the cooled milk and the remaining ingredients making sponge. Let stand. Add creamed mixture to sponge. Add enough flour to knead, the softer the better (about 4 cups). Add fruit mix and raisins. Let rest a few minutes, then knead in fruit. Bake in round loaves on greased cookie sheet at 350 degrees for 45 minutes to 1 hour, depending on size of loaves.

BREADS

The Izaak Walton Inn, located in Essex, Montana, was built in 1939 by the Great Northern Railroad. The original purpose for the Inn was to house rail crews. It is now owned by Larry and Lynda Vielleux. With over 30 kilometers of groomed ski trails, it is the perfect winter destination for cross-country skiers. Located on the southern boundary of Glacier National Park, the Inn in summer is a must see for all vacationers. Amtrak stops about a 1/4 mile from the Inn encouraging rail fans on a year round basis to come "chase trains."

ROCKY MOUNTAIN APPLE BREAD

4 large eggs
2 cups sugar
1/2 cup buttermilk
1/2 cup mayonnaise
1 teaspoon vanilla
3 1/2 cups white flour
1/4 teaspoon salt
1/2 teaspoon baking soda
1 teaspoon baking powder
1 teaspoon ground cinnamon
2 medium size tart green apples
1 cup raisins
1 cup chopped walnuts

In large bowl, beat eggs, sugar, buttermilk, mayonnaise, and vanilla until smooth. In another bowl, mix flour, salt, baking powder, baking soda, and cinnamon. Add to egg mixture and stir just until combined. Core apples and chop. Add to batter with raisins and nuts; stir just to mix. Spread batter evenly in 2 greased and floured 5x9 inch loaf pans. Bake at 375 degrees until a slender wooden pick inserted in center comes out clean, about 1 hour and 10 minutes. Cool in pan for 10 minutes, then turn out onto a rack to cool completely.

Compliments of Izaak Walton Inn

Flathead Lake covers nearly 200 square miles. It is the largest natural fresh water lake in the western United States. It is bordered on the east by the magnificent Mission Range. In the summer months, sail boats, motor boats, and docks make a photographic setting on the clear water.

INGA ANDERSON'S LEFSE
"a Scandinavian tradition in many kitchens"

2 quarts mashed potatoes (4 pounds raw)
1 pint milk (scalded)
1/2 cup butter or margarine, melted
2 teaspoons salt
About 4 cups flour

Mix potatoes, milk, butter, and salt. Chill. To each cup of potatoes, add 1/2 cup flour. Keep mix cold, taking out just enough at a time to roll one on floured surface. Bake lefse on 575 degree lefse griddle. It is rolled like a pie crust and baked on both sides to light brown. Then fold in half and in half again between 2 dish towels until cool. (May be frozen.)

DUMPLINGS

1 cup flour
1 egg
1 1/2 tablespoons oil
2 1/2 teaspoons baking powder
1/2 teaspoon salt
Milk

Add milk to moisten and mix together. Steam 5 minutes. These accompany a pot of beef stew very nicely.

OLD FASHION BAKING POWDER BISCUITS

2 cups flour
1 tablespoon plus 1 teaspoon baking powder
1/2 teaspoon salt
1/4 cup plus 2 tablespoons shortening
2/3 to 3/4 cup milk

Combine flour, baking powder, and salt in bowl. Cut in shortening until mixture resembles coarse meal. Sprinkle milk over flour, stirring lightly with fork until ingredients are evenly moistened. Turn dough out onto lightly floured surface and knead for 1 minute. Roll to 3/4 inch thickness and cut with 2-inch cookie cutter. Place biscuits on lightly greased baking sheet. Bake at 425 degrees for 15 minutes or until lightly browned.

BREADS

The Beartooth Highway stretches from Red Lodge to Yellowstone National Park and is rated as one of the most scenic highways in America. The switch-backs are numerous, the view is spectacular. Pink snow is usually spotted as you near the top. That's right - snowballs in July, only in Montana.

BEST EVER PANCAKES

"serve with homemade syrup"

2 1/2 cups flour
2 teaspoons baking powder
1/4 teaspoon salt
Pinch of baking soda
4 tablespoons sugar
2 cups milk
2 eggs
2 tablespoons melted butter

Mix dry ingredients, add milk, eggs, and butter in order. Beat well. Have your griddle hot to cold water test.

MAPLE SYRUP

1 cup white sugar
1 cup brown sugar
1 cup water
1 teaspoon maple flavoring
1 teaspoon butter
or butter flavoring

Combine sugars and water and bring to a boil over medium heat, boiling 1 minute. Remove from heat and stir in flavoring and butter. Refrigerate leftover syrup.

SIDE DISHES

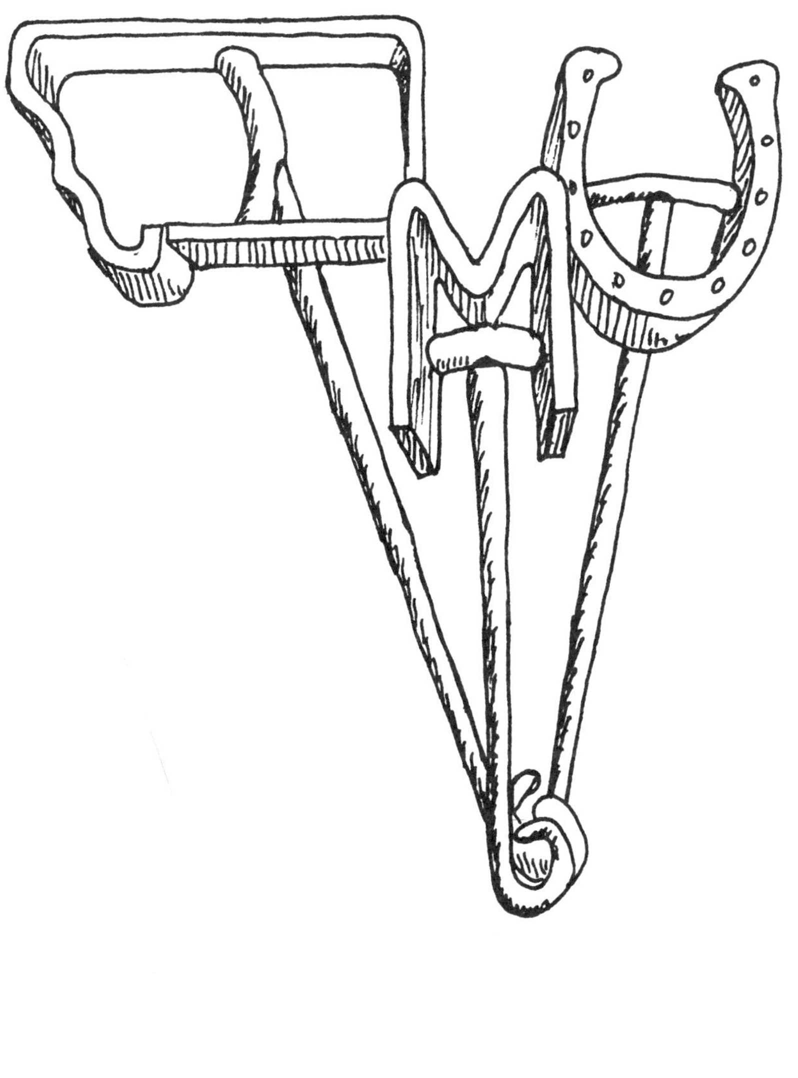

SIDE DISHES

Saturdays in many Montana cities and towns are spent browsing in the Farmers' Markets that are becoming a grower's productive way to end the growing season. Missoula, the Garden City, can boast of having the oldest market in the state and has helped other Montana markets get started.

BROCCOLI CASSEROLE

" a quick and easy hot dish"

1 1/2 cups uncooked rice
2 packages (10-ounce size) chopped broccoli
1 16-ounce jar Cheez Whiz
3/4 cup chopped onion (saute)
3/4 cup chopped celery (saute)
1/2 cup margarine
1 can cream of mushroom soup

Cook rice as directed on box. Add all ingredients in casserole. Bake in 350 degree oven for 40 minutes.

SIDE DISHES

Lieutenant Colonel George Armstrong Custer underestimated the strength of the largest gathering of Sioux and Cheyenne warriors ever on June 25, 1876. Custer and his battalion were massacred on that date and it became known as the Battle of the Little Big Horn. The Little Big Horn National Battlefield is located near Hardin. A re-enactment of the famous conflict takes place in June of each year.

CALICO BEANS

1 pound hamburger
1/2 pound bacon
1 medium onion (chopped)
1 can kidney beans
1 can lima beans
1 can pork and beans
1 cup catsup
3/4 cup brown sugar
1 tablespoon mustard
1 tablespoon vinegar
Salt and pepper

Brown hamburger, bacon and onion. Drain. Add beans with juice from each can. Add last remaining ingredients. Cook in slow oven at 200-250 degrees for at least 3 hours.

When the United States declared war against Spain on April 25, 1898, Montana was authorized by Congress to seek volunteers for one regiment of infantry and one squadron of cavalry. Eligible Montana residents responded 5 times more than the quota set for the state.

HOMEMADE SAUERKRAUT

7-8 pounds shredded cabbage
5-6 tablespoons salt

Remove coarse outer leaves. Wash and shred cabbage fine with sharp knife or cabbage cutter. Do not use coarse ribs or core. In a crock, mix with salt and tamp with wooden spoon or potato masher until crock is filled. Juice should form to cover the cabbage. Cover with a clean white cloth, putting a plate on top weighted down inside crock or jar. Liquid should come up to top of plate. Let stand at room temperature until fermented, about ten days. Remove any scum that forms and wash cloth daily. If there is not enough liquid, dissolve 1 1/2 tablespoons salt in 1 quart of water and add. Process quart jars in boiling water for 20 minutes.

Bibles were first placed in hotel rooms by the Gideons in October of 1908 in the Superior Hotel in Superior, then known an Iron Mountain.

MASHED POTATO CASSEROLE

5 pounds potatoes
1 8-ounce package cream cheese
1 cup half and half
1 teaspoon Lawry's seasoning
1 teaspoon onion salt
1/4 cup margarine
Salt and pepper to taste

Boil potatoes and mash them. Add remaining ingredients and whip. Butter pan or dish. Brush top with butter and sprinkle with paprika. Bake at 350 degrees for 30-45 minutes. Dish can be prepared and frozen.

The Phillips County Fair held in Dodson holds the unique distinction of being the only county fair in Montana that has never missed a year, despite wars, droughts, and other hardships. The first fair was held October 5-7, 1915. One of the main attractions was an Angora cat and her four kittens.

ZUCCHINI CASSEROLE

6 cups zucchini cubed (peeled)
1 cup sour cream
1 cup grated carrots
1 can cream of chicken soup
1/2 cup chopped onion
1/2 cup margarine (melted)
1 box stuffing mix (chicken flavored)

Precook zucchini cubes in salt water for 5 minutes, drain. Mix sour cream and soup, add carrots, zucchini, and onion. In a greased casserole, mix dressing with melted butter, saving small amount of dressing to sprinkle on top. Fold in vegetable mix. Sprinkle on remaining stuffing mix. Bake for 30-40 minutes in 325 degree oven.

SIDE DISHES

Senator Mike Mansfield, a graduate of the University of Montana, was elected to Congress in 1942. He won election to the Senate in 1952, serving as a majority leader from 1961 to 1977, holding that position longer than any other person in American History. Senator Mansfield retired after serving 11 years as U.S. Ambassador to Japan, an appointment by President Jimmy Carter.

POTATO PARTY CASSEROLE

1/4 teaspoon salt
2 tablespoons chopped onion
1 can cream of chicken soup
1 pint sour cream
1 32-ounce bag frozen hash browns
3/4 cup melted butter
2 cups grated cheese (American)
2 cups crushed cornflakes

Defrost potatoes. Combine 1/2 cup melted butter with all ingredients except cornflakes. Pour into 9x13 inch pan. Mix the remaining butter with cornflakes and sprinkle over potato mixture. Bake at 350 degrees for 1 1/2 hours.

Nelson Story is known for bringing the first longhorns into Montana from Texas. He purchased 1,000 head of cattle at $4.60 apiece. With hired hands and his herd, he headed for Montana arriving in December of 1866, locating near Livingston.

EVELYN'S GOURMET POTATOES

- **6 medium potatoes, boiled with skins**
- **3 cups shredded Cheddar cheese**
- **1/4 cup butter**
- **1 1/2 cups sour cream, room temperature**
- **1/3 cup chopped green onions**
- **1 teaspoon salt**
- **1/4 teaspoon pepper**
- **2 tablespoons butter**

Cook potatoes in skins. Cool, peel, and crumble. In saucepan over low heat, combine cheese and butter. Stir occasionally until mostly melted. Remove from heat. Blend onion, salt, pepper, and sour cream. Fold in potatoes. Pour into greased 2-quart casserole. Dot with 2 tablespoons butter. Bake at 325 degrees for 25 minutes, uncovered.

The town of Bridger was named after Jim Bridger, one of the first white men to explore Yellowstone Park. There was a popular belief that he could map any part of the Rocky Mountains from memory and Bridger, himself, boasted he could smell his way when he couldn't see it.

BROCCOLI CORN BAKE

1 16-ounce can of cream style corn
1 10-ounce package frozen broccoli
1 egg, beaten
1/2 teaspoon salt
Dash of pepper
1/2 cup coarse saltine cracker crumbs
1 tablespoon minced onion
2 tablespoons melted butter

Combine the ingredients and place in 1-quart buttered casserole. Combine **1/4 cup cracker crumbs (6 crackers)** with **1 tablespoon melted butter.** Sprinkle over vegetable mix. Bake uncovered at 350 degrees for 35-40 minutes.

Montana tried for statehood three times before being admitted to the Union in 1889. The first attempt was in 1866 but the state's population was below the required 60,000. The second failure was in 1884 due to party politics. In October, 1889, Montana voters approved the new state constitution and on November 8, 1889, Montana became the forty-first state in the Union.

EMERSON FAMILY SCALLOPED OYSTERS

1 quart oysters
2 cups milk
1 teaspoon salt
1 cup melted butter
4 cups cracker crumbs
Few dashes of pepper

Wash and drain oysters, using small eastern oysters if possible. Mix oysters, milk, salt and pepper. Mix butter and cracker crumbs. Put layer of oysters, then cracker crumbs, making three layers. Add a little milk on top if needed. Bake 30 minutes at 450 degrees.

SIDE DISHES

Cowboys and cowgirls have gathered in Big Timber and Lewistown each summer since 1986 to participate in the annual Montana Cowboy Poetry Gathering. Cowboy poetry is about the life in a cowboy's world, the courage it takes to survive, and sometimes about a cowboy's sweetheart. These folks keep the West alive through their poetry and lyrics. Mosey on over to Lewistown about the third week in August, it's located in the middle of Montana.

BAKED BEANS

1 can kidney beans
1 large can pork and beans
1 can butter beans
8 strips bacon
1 onion, chopped
Shake of garlic salt
1 teaspoon dry mustard
1/4 cup vinegar
1/2 cup brown sugar

Fry bacon until crisp. Add onion, garlic salt, mustard, and vinegar. Simmer about 15 minutes. Add beans and brown sugar. Bake 1 1/4 hours at 350 degrees.

PERSONAL FAVORITES

Notes & Recipes:

Main Dishes

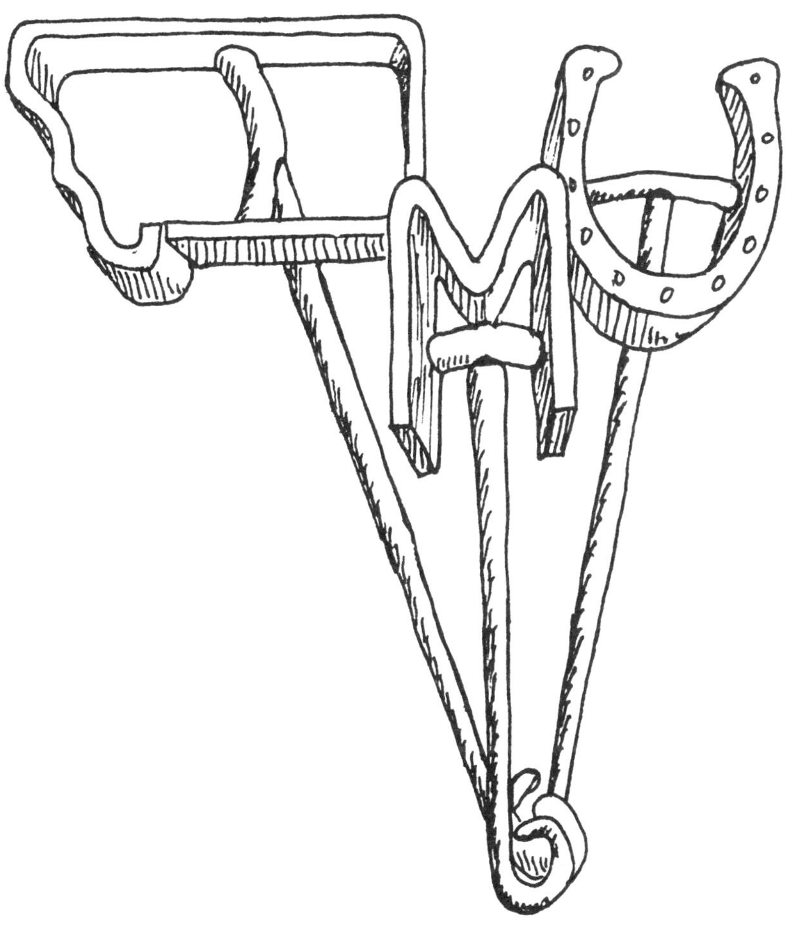

The Shields River is located west of the Crazy Mountains near Wilsall and Clyde Park. It empties into the Yellowstone River near Livingston. The Shields River was named after John Shields, one of the members of the Lewis and Clark party.

ETHEL'S BAKED SALMON BISCAYNE

3 tablespoons butter
3 tablespoons flour
1 cup milk
1 cup flaked salmon
1 tablespoon minced parsley
Dash of salt and pepper
1 tablespoon lemon juice
3 eggs, slightly beaten

Melt butter. Blend in flour; gradually add milk, stirring until thick and smooth. Add seasonings. Combine salmon, lemon juice, and parsley. Add to first mixture with beaten eggs. Turn into greased loaf pan and set in pan of hot water. Bake at 350 degrees until firm, about 30 minutes.

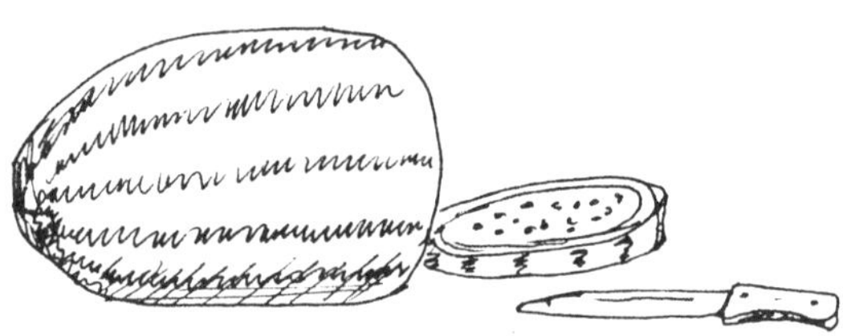

"Blue Ribbon Trout Streams" is a phrase you hear often in Montana and these streams are recognized for this "Blue Ribbon" by the quality of water and excellence of the fish; although there is no set classification. There are over 400 miles of Blue Ribbon trout fishing and just to name a few of the rivers that claim this prize are parts of the Madison, Jefferson, Gallatin, Big Hole, Clark Fork, Yellowstone, and the Big Horn. The professionals say anyone can catch a trout in Montana's streams so pack up and head for one of these world wide acclaimed fishing spots.

BILL SERRETTE'S PAN FRIED TROUT

Fresh Mountain Trout
Salt and pepper
Pancake flour, cornmeal or flour
Vegetable oil

Trout should be moist. Remove heads from trout if desired. Larger trout should be split in half down the backbone for cooking. Sprinkle trout with salt and pepper on both sides and in body cavity. Also sprinkle salt and pepper on flour coating to be used. Roll trout in flour just before cooking and place in hot fry pan or grill with vegetable oil 1/8 inch deep. Cook over medium heat until golden brown. Turn carefully and brown other side. (Approximately 5 minutes on each side.) Drain oil off fish on absorbent paper and place on hot plate. Serve trout while hot.

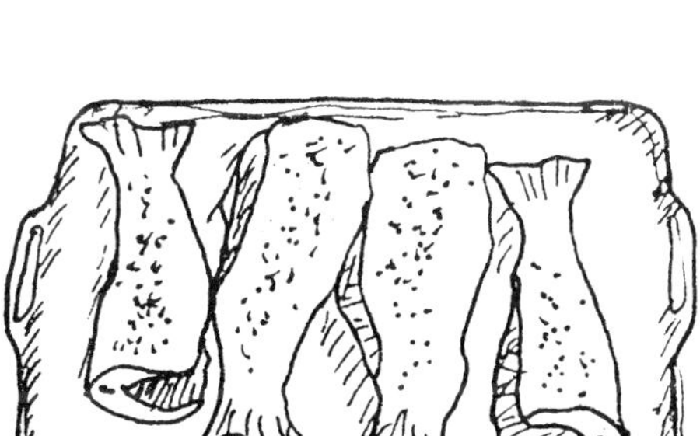

MAIN DISHES

"From where the sun now stands, I will fight no more forever" were the words spoken by Chief Joseph as he surrendered his band of Nez Perce to Colonel Nelson Miles in October of 1877. Located about 17 miles south of where Chinook exists today is the site of the last major armed conflict between Indian people and the U.S. Army. The Nez Perce hold a memorial at the battleground each year.

BREADED FISH FILLETS

3 cups herb croutons, crushed (about 1 cup)
1/2 cup grated Parmesan cheese
1/2 teaspoon paprika
2 pounds fillet of sole (thawed)
1/2 cup milk
1/4 cup melted butter

Toss herb crumbs with cheese and paprika. Dip fillets in milk, then in crumbs. Place fish in a 9x13 inch buttered baking dish. Drizzle with melted butter. Bake in 500 degree oven for 10-12 minutes until fish flakes easily. Serve with tartar sauce.

A dinosaur find has been located 12 miles outside of Choteau. The discovery includes baby and adult duck-billed dinosaurs. Numerous pieces of other dinosaurs and fossilized creatures also were found and are on display at the Old Trail Museum. The dig has drawn world-wide attention and a Dinosaur Day is a summer event scheduled each June in Choteau.

TUNA CASSEROLE

1 large can Chinese noodles
1 can tuna, drained
1 can sliced water chestnuts, drained
1 can cream of mushroom soup
1 cup celery, sliced
1 cup diced onion
1 tablespoon soy sauce
1/4 cup water
1/2 cup cashew nuts or sliced almonds

Cook celery and onion in small amount of oil until lightly cooked. Mix soup, water, tuna, soy sauce, onions, celery, and water chestnuts. Spread half of noodles in buttered baking dish. Cover with tuna mixture. Top with remaining noodles. Sprinkle nuts on top. Bake 30 minutes at 350 degrees.

When the Lewis and Clark exhibition arrived back in St. Louis in 1806, the news of their findings spread excitement and high interest. Manuel Lisa, a fur trader from New Orleans, quickly gathered together a party of trappers and traveled up the Missouri and Yellowstone Rivers. In 1807, Lisa built the first fur post in Montana at the junction of the Big Horn and Yellowstone Rivers.

SHRIMP CASSEROLE

2 cups cooked rice
1 can green asparagus spears, drained
1 8-ounce can medium shrimp
1 can cream of mushroom soup
3/4 cup milk
Salt and pepper
1 tablespoon chopped pimento
1 cup grated American cheese

Place rice in greased 8x8 inch baking dish. Place asparagus over rice. Top with shrimp. Mix salt, pepper, soup, milk, and pimento; pour over shrimp. Sprinkle with cheese. Bake at 400 degrees for 35 minutes.

MARINATED CHICKEN BREASTS

8 chicken breasts
1 package dried beef
Salt and pepper to taste
Bacon
1 can cream of mushroom soup
1 small carton sour cream

Skin, split, and debone chicken breasts. Line a 9x13 inch pan with dried beef. Season breasts with salt and pepper; wrap in bacon and place on beef. Mix soup and sour cream; spread over chicken. Cover with plastic wrap and refrigerate at least 24 hours. Uncover and bake 2 hours at 300 degrees.

Fort Benton, one of Montana's oldest communities, played an important part in Montana's early days as it was located at the head of navigation on the Missouri River. Because of its location, all of the cargo had to be unloaded there and then distributed to the gold camps.

BARBECUED CHICKEN

1 medium size onion, chopped
1 tablespoon oil
1/2 cup catsup
3 tablespoons brown sugar
2 tablespoons vinegar
1 1/2 teaspoons Worcestershire sauce
1/2 teaspoons each: salt, celery salt, and chili powder
1/2 cup water
1 chicken, about 3 pounds, cut up

In large skillet, saute onion in oil until tender. Add catsup, sugar, vinegar, Worcestershire sauce, water, salt, celery salt, and chili powder. Bring to boil. Add chicken. Cover and simmer for 1 hour. Uncover; simmer 15 minutes longer or until chicken is tender, turning pieces from time to time.

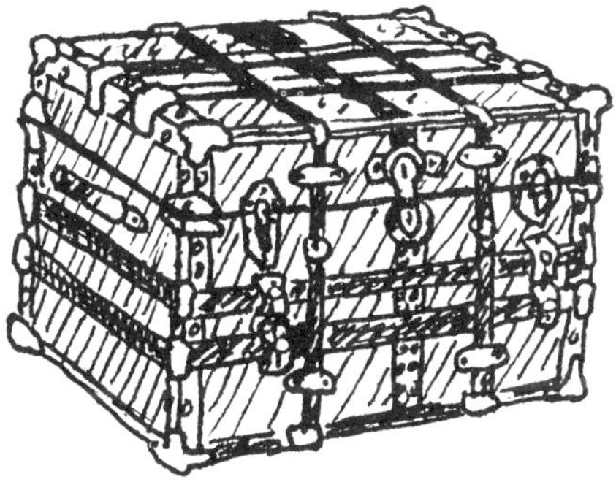

Wild turkey hunting in Montana opens in the spring of the year, usually lasting about one month. Turkeys are expanding in population and are now found all across the state. Ponderosa pine and cottonwood bottoms along rivers and creeks are the suitable habitats.

CHICKEN OR TURKEY CASSEROLE

"what to do with leftovers"

2 cups cooked chicken or turkey
1 1/2 cups spaghetti, broken into inch pieces, cooked
1/4 cup chopped green pepper
1/4 cup chopped onion
1/2 teaspoon salt
1/2 teaspoon pepper
1 can cream of mushroom soup
1 cup turkey or chicken broth
1 1/2 cups sharp Cheddar cheese, grated
1/2 cup pimento (optional)
1 cup buttered bread crumbs

Cut chicken or turkey into bite size pieces. Mix all ingredients together, covering with buttered crumbs. Bake for 1 hour at 350 degrees. This dish can be prepared early in the day and refrigerated until time to bake.

The Yellowstone National Park fires of 1988 burned nearly 1,000,000 acres. Thousands of fire fighters were called to work, along with several aircrafts to fight these terrible fires. The disaster was caused by lighting, strong winds, and the worst drought in history.

SPICED PEACH CHICKEN

"a tasty dish to serve with plain or wild rice"

1 fryer (cut up)
Coat chicken with flour. Brown in butter in skillet. Remove.
Saute **1/2 cup of chopped onion** in skillet until limp.

Mix and add:
2 cups orange juice
4 tablespoons brown sugar
4 tablespoons apple cider vinegar
1/2 teaspoon mace
1 teaspoon ginger
1 can peaches with juice. (An extra can of peaches may be added if you prefer a bit more fruit).

Chicken can be returned to skillet to finish cooking or you can put in shallow pan and put in oven. Pour sauce mixture over chicken. Serve with rice.

Skillet: Cook 30-45 minutes.
Oven: Bake at 350-375 degrees for 30-45 minutes.

Billings, the Magic City, sits below the majestic Rimrocks. It is the largest metropolitan area in Montana and is populated with over 100,000 friendly, spirited Montanans.

QUICK SAUCY CHICKEN STIR FRY

2 tablespoons oil
1 cup broccoli flowerets
1 cup cauliflowerets
3/4 cup 2-inch julienne cut carrots
1/4 cup green onions, sliced
1 clove garlic
1 tablespoon soy sauce
1/2 teaspoon ginger
3 chicken breast halves, skinned boned, and cut into 1-inch pieces
1/2 cup mayonnaise (Miracle Whip)

Stir fry vegetables in 1 tablespoon oil, remove when nearly tender. Add 1 tablespoon oil and stir fry chicken until tender. Return vegetables and combine remaining ingredients. Mix well and serve over rice.

MAIN DISHES

The Old Tractor Club of Sheridan County has a display of threshing machines and tractors located at the Daniels County Fairgrounds in Scobey. It is said to be one of the most outstanding collections around, featuring a "Sunshine" combine, one of the earliest self-propelled combines built.

CHICKEN AND RICE HOT DISH

1 small package Minute Rice (4 1/2 ounces)
1 can cream of celery soup
1 can cream of mushroom soup
1/2 cup milk
1 envelope dry onion soup mix
1 cut up frying chicken

Grease 9x13 inch baking dish. Sprinkle rice over bottom of dish. Heat soup and milk, stir until blended. Pour over raw rice; place chicken over top and sprinkle onion soup on top. Seal pan with foil and bake at 325 degrees at least 2 hours.

MAIN DISHES

The Greycliff Prairie Dog Town is open 24 hours year round. These "dogs" live in colonies of several hundred acres. Other wildlife frequent the "Town" such as western meadowlarks, badgers, desert cottontails, and the endangered black-footed ferret.

CHICKEN ENCHILADAS

Corn tortillas cut in bite-size pieces
3-4 cups diced cooked chicken
1 small can green chilies
Chopped green onions
1 cup grated Cheddar cheese
1 can cream of mushroom soup, warmed
1 can cream of chicken soup, warmed

Layer ingredients in order given in 9x13 inch pan, reserving some cheese for topping. Top last layer with reserved cheese. Bake uncovered at 350 degrees for 45 minutes.

CHALUPES

5 pound lean pork roast
2 pounds dry pinto beans (soak beans overnight)

In large roasting pan, mix the following:

4 buttons of garlic, chopped fine
4 tablespoons chili powder
4 tablespoons cumin seeds or 2 tablespoons cumin powder
3 tablespoons salt
4 tablespoons oregano
4 Jalapeno peppers, chopped

Add a little water to mix the above spices.

Add pork roast and beans. Cover with hot water. Cook for 4-6 hours on top of stove, always adding hot water when needed. Simmer. As pork cooks, debone roast and cut meat fine. Cook to the consistency of thick chili. Serve with corn chips for bottom layer of plate. Add the condiments as individuals prefer.

Condiments:
Grated Cheddar cheese
Chopped onion
Chopped tomatoes
Chopped radishes
Chopped green peppers
Mashed avocado
Shredded lettuce
Hot sauce to taste

Hot Sauce:
1 small can green taco sauce
1 tablespoon Tabasco sauce
1 garlic bud
Salt and pepper to taste
1 medium onion, chopped fine
1 can (15 ounce) tomatoes
4 Jalapeno peppers, chopped

Serve the above in individual dishes.

Hot Sauce Directions:
Mix in blender until all items are blended. May be stored for a long period of time under refrigeration. Excellent on Mexican foods.

MAIN DISHES

Old Time Fiddler Contests are held throughout Montana about anytime of the year. Fiddlers, young and old, fiddle away into the wee hours of the morning and everybody's feet keep time with the music as the judges go about picken' a winner.

BURRITOS

12 flour tortillas
2 pounds hamburger
2 cans mashed pinto or small red beans, undrained
1 large chopped onion
2 cups Cheddar cheese
1 teaspoon garlic powder
1 teaspoon chili powder
Salt to taste

Brown hamburger and drain off grease, then add the rest of the ingredients. Fill flour tortillas and fry or top with favorite sauce and bake at 350 degrees until heated well, about 30 minutes.

MAIN DISHES

With the rich grass lands of Montana fast becoming grazing land for herds of cattle, the cattle rustlers became active throughout the state in the early 1880's. Cowmen formed the Montana Stockgrower's Association in Miles City on April 3, 1885 to do battle against the notorious outlaws.

GOULASH
"an old favorite"

1 pound hamburger
1 small onion, chopped
1/2 green pepper, chopped
1 small can mushrooms
1 can tomato soup
1 can cream style corn
1/4 pound spaghetti, cooked
1/2 cup grated cheese
Sprinkle of paprika

Brown hamburger, add onion and pepper. Add remaining ingredients. Mix together and pour into casserole dish. Put grated cheese and paprika on top and bake at 350 degrees for 30 minutes.

MAIN DISHES

Ranches, small farms, and feedlots produce top choice beef in Montana. You can stride into an eatery, hang your hat, and order up a steak. You can bet it will be a big one. In some places, if you eat all of the first serving, you get the second steak free. Now, there's a deal, pardner!

CHICKEN FRIED STEAK

1 1/2 pounds pounded round steak
Salt and pepper
2/3 cup flour
1/2 teaspoon paprika
1/2 teaspoon salt
1/4 teaspoon poultry seasoning
2 eggs, beaten

Cut steak into four pieces and season with salt and pepper. Combine flour and seasonings. Dip meat in egg and then in seasoned flour. Fry steaks in hot oil until browned on each side. Make cream gravy, if desired.

SLOW BAKE LASAGNA

1 1/2 pounds ground beef
1 12-ounce can tomato paste
2 8-ounce cans tomato sauce
1 16-ounce can tomatoes
1 tablespoon parsley
1 teaspoon oregano
2 bay leaves
1 pound mozzarella cheese
2 8-ounce packages cream cheese, sliced lengthwise
Lasagna noodles

Brown hamburger, add spices, tomato paste, tomato sauce, and tomatoes. Simmer for 3-4 hours. (A crock pot is convenient for simmering the sauce.)

Cook the noodles (about 12) according to directions on package. Put a small amount of sauce in bottom of 9x13 inch pan, layer on three or four noodles. Add about 1/3 of the sauce mixture, next mozzarella cheese and then a few slices of cream cheese. Continue repeating the layers; ending up with sprinkling mozzarella on top for last layer. Bake at 350 degrees for 1/2 hour.

KITTY'S LASAGNE ROLLS WITH SPINACH SAUCE

Sauce:
2 tablespoons margarine
2 tablespoons onion, finely chopped
Scant 1/2 teaspoon garlic, minced
2 tablespoons flour
1 1/4 cups milk
1/4 cup plus 2 tablespoons grated Parmesan cheese, divided
1/2 teaspoon salt, divided
1/4 teaspoon pepper, divided
Dash of nutmeg
1/2 teaspoon marjoram
1/4 teaspoon basil

1 10-ounce package frozen chopped spinach, cooked and drained thoroughly
1 15-ounce container ricotta cheese
1 8-ounce package mozzarella cheese, shredded
1 egg
12 lasagne noodles (about 8-ounces) cooked and drained (boil just 6 minutes)

In medium saucepan, melt better; add onion and garlic and saute 3 minutes or until onions are soft. Stir in flour; cook 1 minute. Add milk and stir over medium heat until thickened. Stir in 2 tablespoons Parmesan cheese, 1/4 teaspoon salt, 1/8 teaspoon pepper and nutmeg. Pour sauce into blender and add 1/2 spinach; puree until smooth. Pour sauce back into sauce pan; stir in remaining spinach. Pour 1/2 cup sauce into deep 3-quart casserole. In large bowl, combine ricotta, mozzarella, and 1/4 cup Parmesan cheese, egg, herbs, 1/4 teaspoon salt and 1/8 teaspoon pepper.

To assemble - lay noodles out flat. Spread 3 tablespoons cheese mixture over each, leaving 2 inches of noodle uncovered at one end. Starting at opposite end, roll up jelly roll style. Stand upright in casserole dish. Arrange rolls to touch each other. Pour remaining sauce over rolls. Bake uncovered for 30 minutes or until heated through at 350 degrees. Serves 12.

The Northern Lights brighten northern Montana skies, with their best show usually occurring in March, April, September, and October; depending upon the time of greatest sunspot activity. Green is the most common color seen during the display.

BEEF SHORT RIB BARBEQUE

3 or 4 pounds beef short ribs
2 tablespoons fat for browning
1 package dry onion soup mix
1/4 cup vinegar
2 tablespoons brown sugar
1 cup catsup
1/2 cup water
1 teaspoon salt
1 teaspoon prepared mustard

Heat fat in dutch oven and brown ribs well on all sides. Combine all other ingredients in mixing bowl and pour over meat. Cover with tight lid and simmer for 2 hours, or until meat is tender, turning now and then.

MAIN DISHES

When gold was discovered in southwestern Montana in 1862, eager prospectors rushed to the area. They soon realized that gold also brought problems. Outlaws spread terror in the mining camps. Groups of citizens took the law into their own hands and formed the Vigilantes. They adopted the symbol 3-7-77. Many outlaws were hung, including the Henry Plummer gang in 1864, and many left the area in fear for their lives.

SHIPWRECK STEW

Layer all vegetables and meat raw in a casserole or 9x13 inch pan.

4 medium sized potatoes, pared and diced
2 medium onions, chopped
1/2 cup celery, chopped
1 cup instant rice, uncooked
1 can kidney beans
1 1/2 pounds ground beef
1 can tomato soup

Bake covered at 350 degrees for 1 hour and 15 minutes, uncovering the last 15 minutes of baking.

MAIN DISHES

Some famous movie actors and actresses have been born in Montana, including Myrna Loy (Radersburg); George Montgomery (Brady); and Gary Cooper (Helena). Many other celebrities have moved to the Big Sky and made Montana their adopted state.

CROCK POT BEEF

2 pounds cubed steak or stew meat
1 can cream of mushroom soup
1 can cream of celery soup
1/2 package onion soup mix (use whole package for more flavor)
Noodles

Brown meat and combine with soups and onion soup mix. Put in crock pot and cook 8 hours or until meat is tender. Cook noodles and combine with meat or serve meat over noodles. You may use as many noodles as you wish. Do not salt noodles when you cook them.

<u>**Oven Method:**</u>
Brown meat and put just enough water to cook and bake in oven until meat is tender. Add soups and onion soup mix and cooked noodles and bake one hour at 300 degrees.

Reedpoint hosted its first sheep drive on Labor Day, 1989; the year of the state's 100th birthday. It has continued annually since and entertains thousands of people. Hundreds of sheep make their entrance and trample down Main Street. The Montana Wool Grower's Association holds a wool demonstration. Other festivities include a parade and street dance. Sheep shearing and sheep dog trials are also on the docket, along with foods and crafts and the ever popular sheep drive T-shirts.

SHEEPHERDER'S CASSEROLE

6 or 7 potatoes
1 onion, sliced
Salt and pepper
1 pound hamburger
1 can Cheddar cheese soup
1 can milk
Sliced pepperoni
1 can tomato soup
1 teaspoon sugar
1/2 teaspoon oregano
1/2 cup chopped onion
1 teaspoon red pepper
Mozzarella cheese

Peel and slice potatoes and place potatoes and onion in a greased 9x13 inch pan. Salt and pepper. Brown hamburger and pour over potatoes. Heat Cheddar cheese soup and milk, pour over hamburger. Layer pepperoni over hamburger mixture. Mix together tomato soup, sugar, oregano, 1/2 cup onion and red pepper. Pour over pepperoni. Cover with foil. Bake at 400 degrees for 15 minutes. Reduce heat to 350 degrees. Bake 50-60 minutes. Remove foil and sprinkle with mozzarella cheese. Return to oven until cheese melts.

MOM'S CHILI
"a cold winter's night special"

1 large onion, chopped
1 green pepper, chopped
2 pounds ground beef
1 large can of tomatoes
3 cans kidney beans
Chili powder to taste

Brown onion, pepper and beef in dutch oven or large skillet. Add cut up tomatoes and simmer for 2 hours. Add beans, simmer for 1 hour. Season with chili powder. Best when made the day before.

COWBOY STEW IN A PIE

1 pound ground beef
2 cups sliced potatoes
2 cups sliced carrots
1 green pepper, sliced
1 medium onion, sliced
3 stalks celery, sliced
Salt and pepper to taste
1 can tomato soup

Arrange vegetables in layers, in buttered casserole. Add salt and pepper to each layer. Season meat and press out to form a cover over vegetables. Pour tomato soup over meat. Bake, covered at 350 degrees, for 1 1/2 hours or until potatoes are done.

The Great Northern Railway was one of the nation's most successful railroads. It provided needed transportation through Montana. Jim Hill, nicknamed the "Empire Builder", was its developer. His railroad extended from the Great Lakes to the Pacific Ocean. After years of service, it combined with two other railroads; the Northern Pacific and Burlington. The new railroad has since been named the Burlington Northern.

SLOPPY JOES

"serves 15-20"

8 pounds hamburger
6 green peppers
6 medium onions
1/2 gallon catsup
(four bottles)
1/2 cup dry mustard
1/2 cup sugar
1/2 cup cider vinegar
A hint of celery salt
Salt and pepper

Brown hamburger, onions, and peppers in vegetable oil. Add other ingredients and simmer for at least 30 minutes, stirring occasionally to keep from scorching. Spoon into warmed hamburger buns. Double for larger crowd.

Cattle ranching began in the Deer Lodge Valley in the late 1850's. Johnny Grant settled there and in less than a decade he had built a herd of 2,000 cattle. He later moved his ranching operation close to Deer Lodge and eventually sold out to Conrad Kohrs. Kohrs built an empire in cattle. Going into partnership with John Bielenberg, their cattle were some of the best that grazed Montana's grasslands. The Grant-Kohrs Ranch is a National Historic Site, the former home of the state's "Cattle King".

MONTANA BEEF STROGANOFF

1 pound sirloin steak
Flour for dredging and thickening
Salt
2 tablespoons margarine
1 3-ounce can mushrooms, drained
1/2 cup chopped onion
A shake of garlic
1 tablespoon tomato paste
1 10-ounce can condensed beef broth
1 cup dairy sour cream
2 tablespoons dry white wine

Cut meat into 1/4 inch strips. Combine 1 tablespoon flour and 1/2 teaspoon salt, coat meat. Heat skillet and add margarine. When melted add meat strips and brown quickly on both sides. Add mushrooms, chopped onion, and a shake of garlic. Cook 3-4 minutes or until onion is crisp and tender. Remove meat and mushrooms from pan. Add 2 tablespoons margarine to pan drippings, blend in 3 tablespoons flour. Add tomato paste. Stir in beef broth. Cook and stir over medium heat until thick and bubbly. Return browned meat and mushrooms to skillet. Stir in sour cream and wine. Cook slowly until heated through. Serve over hot buttered noodles. Serves 4-5.

MAIN DISHES

The cowboy became a prominent figure in Montana's history. The chaps, the kerchief, the wide brim hat, and boots were part of the get-up they wore as they drove the cattle and kept guard over them at night. Roundups were another part of the business and it was a time when the cowboys could exhibit their skills in riding and roping and trading stories with other yarn-spinners around the campfire.

OVEN STEAK STROGANOFF

2 pounds round steak, pounded with flour
1 teaspoon salt
1/4 teaspoon pepper
6 medium potatoes, sliced 1/2 inch thick
1 medium onion, sliced
1 4-1/2 ounce can mushrooms (optional)
1 can cream of mushroom soup
1 cup dairy sour cream
2 tablespoons catsup

Place meat in 9x13 inch pan. Season with **1/2 teaspoon salt** and **1/8 teaspoon pepper**. Place onion slices on meat, and layer on potato slices. Mix soup, sour cream, catsup, 1/2 teaspoon salt, 1/8 teaspoon pepper. Add mushrooms. Spread over all and cover with foil to seal. Bake at 350 degrees for 2-2 1/2 hours.

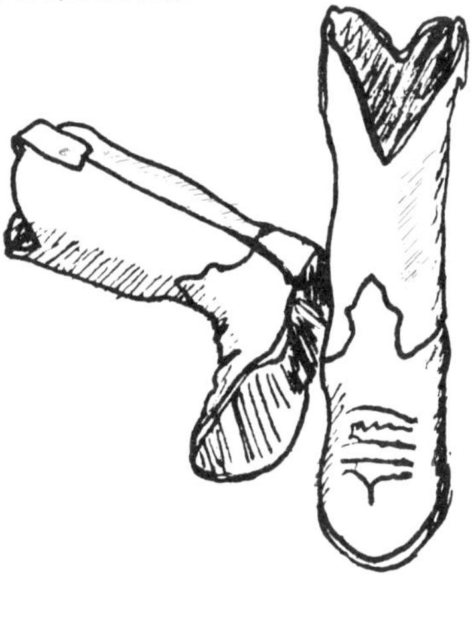

MAIN DISHES

In the 1860's, Virginia City became a melting pot as gold seekers came from nearly every state in the union as well as Germany, China and other foreign countries. They had visions of becoming wealthy but only a small percentage acquired that dream.

ORIENTAL HAMBURGER CASSEROLE

1 pound hamburger (browned)
1 medium chopped onion
2 tablespoons margarine
1 cup chopped celery

Mix:
1 can cream of mushroom soup
1 can cream of chicken soup
1 can water
2 tablespoons soy sauce

Add:
1 cup uncooked minute rice
1 can water chestnuts
1 can bean sprouts

Combine first four ingredients in casserole. Add the soup mixture and next the rice, water chestnuts, and bean sprouts. Bake for 25 minutes at 350 degrees. Remove from oven and top with one large can Chinese noodles. Bake 15 minutes longer.

NORWEGIAN MEATBALLS

"a Christmas Eve tradition"

Ingredients	6 Servings	24 Servings
Lean ground beef	1 pound	4 pounds
Eggs	1	4
Cracker crumbs	6 tablespoons	1 1/2 cups
Milk	1/4 cup	1 cup
Celery salt	3/4 teaspoon	1 teaspoon
Pepper	1/4 teaspoon	1 teaspoon
Ground nutmeg	1/8 teaspoon	1/4 teaspoon
Minced onion	1 tablespoon	1/4 cup
Butter or margarine	2 tablespoons	1/3 cup
Flour	1 tablespoon	1/4 cup
Beef broth	1 cup	4 cups

For 6 servings: In a large bowl; beat beef, eggs, crumbs, milk, celery salt, pepper, nutmeg, and onion with electric mixer at high speed until mixture is very smooth and light. Dip hands in cold water and shape meat mixture into 1-inch balls. Melt butter in large skillet over medium heat. Add meatballs without crowding and cook until browned, shaking pan occasionally to brown evenly. Remove from skillet with slotted spoon. Stir flour into pan drippings until smooth. Cook 3 minutes until browned, stirring constantly. Stir in broth and cook, stirring until slightly thickened. Return meatballs to skillet. Reduce heat; cover and simmer about 15 minutes or until meatballs are cooked through. The meatballs can also be put into a roasting pan and baked in the oven for one hour rather than the skillet method. You may also add more broth and thickening for more gravy.

For 24: Mix the meat mixture in 2 batches. When smooth and light, put into large bowl and mix well with a wooden spoon or with hands. Proceed as above.

At the end of main street in Deer Lodge stands the first territorial prison in the western United States. The structure was built by convict labor with construction beginning in 1870. It was completed in 1871 with fourteen cells that soon filled with territorial and federal criminals. The Old Montana Prison complex now accommodates the Powell County Museum and the Towe Ford Museum, which displays more than eighty old cars. A new prison has since been built on the outskirts of town, closing the historic site for "outlaw business" in 1979.

APPLESAUCE MEATBALLS

1 egg
1/2 cup milk
1 1/2 cups herb seasoned stuffing croutons
1 1/2 pounds ground beef
2/3 cup applesauce
3 teaspoons chopped onion
1/2 cup water (or more)
1 can cream of tomato soup
Salt and pepper

Beat egg and milk, add croutons. Let stand 5 minutes or until soft. Beat until soft. Add meat, applesauce, onion and seasoning. Mix thoroughly. Shape into 24 balls. Brown in small amount of oil in skillet. Add soup and water and simmer for about 30 minutes. These meatballs can also be baked in a casserole for 45 minutes at 350 degrees.

MAIN DISHES

Between 1900 and 1918, towns were springing up all over Montana and the population grew. "County-busting" became a political game and with The Leighton Act of 1911, Montana now has fifty-six counties. Before that time there were twenty-eight.

SIGERT'S MEATBALLS

2 pounds ground lean beef
1 pound ground lean pork
2 eggs
2 cups crumbled Corn Flakes or Wheaties
1 tablespoon onion juice
1 teaspoon nutmeg
1/4 teaspoon pepper
Lawry's seasoned salt to taste

Mix all ingredients. Shape into balls about the size of a walnut. Brown in butter then simmer in potato water for about 1/2 hour.

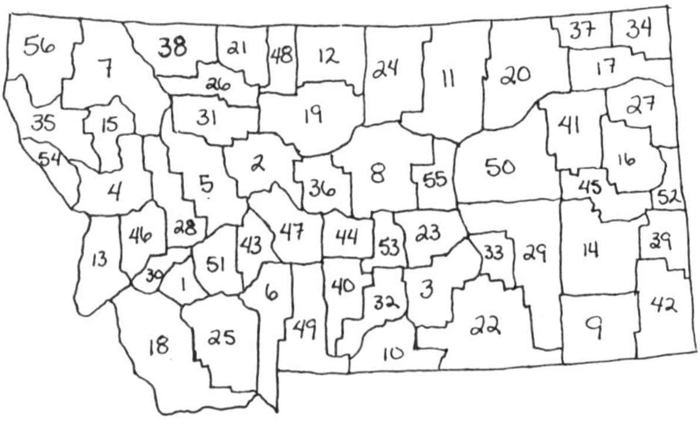

MAIN DISHES

John James Audubon arrived in Montana in 1843 to do a study on the birds of the area. His studies became valuable input in describing the early period of the state.

ITALIAN MEATBALLS

Tomato Basil Sauce:
1/2 cup chopped onion
3 minced garlic
1 1/2 teaspoons dried basil leaves
3/4 teaspoon dried oregano
3/4 teaspoon fennel seed, crushed
3 cups tomato sauce
1 can (16 ounce) tomatoes, drained and chopped
Salt and pepper to taste

Mix above ingredients, bring to a boil, reduce heat and simmer for 5 minutes.

1 pound lean ground beef
1/2 pound bulk pork sausage
1/2 cup chopped onion
1/2 cup dry unseasoned bread crumbs
1 egg
1/4 teaspoon pepper

Mix beef and sausage well. Add remaining ingredients, shape into meatballs. Barbecue the meatballs on the grill for about 20 minutes, brushing them frequently with sauce.

Raising cattle is one of the chief industries in Montana. Cattle ranches spread over much of the state. Beginning in the 1870's, long cattle drives brought herds from overstocked ranges as far away as Texas to be fattened up on Montana ranges and then shipped to market.

BOB'S MONTANA MEAT LOAF

2 pounds ground beef
1 1/2 cups bread crumbs
3/4 cup milk
1/4 cup catsup
2 eggs
1 package dry onion soup mix
1 small can mushrooms

Mix ingredients and put in a casserole dish. Bake 1 1/2 hours at 325 degrees.

MAIN DISHES

Most of Montana became a part of the United States when President Thomas Jefferson purchased Louisiana from France in 1803. Louisiana being land stretching west and north of New Orleans, 800,000 square miles, which in later years would become a part of the state of Montana. Meriwether Lewis and William Clark, chosen by President Jefferson, set off from St. Louis to explore the purchase on May 14, 1804; arriving back in St. Louis on September 23, 1806. This marked the most impressive explorations in American and Montana history.

DELICIOUS DINNER IN A "PINCH"

1 frozen roast (any size, any cut)
1 package onion soup mix
1 cup water
6 potatoes with skins, quartered
6 carrots, cut in 4 inch lengths

Put frozen roast in large pan, sprinkle soup over top and add the water. Cover with foil and put in 225 degree oven first thing in the morning. Add potatoes and carrots at noon. Tender and delicious by dinner time. Make gravy out of juice, if you desire.

On a hill overlooking Fort Benton is a monument erected by the Great Northern Railroad employees in the memory of "Shep". Shep was a collie devoted to his master, a sheepherder who died in 1936. The remains were taken to the depot and shipped back East for burial. For almost six years, Shep met every train, looking for his master to return. In January of 1942, Shep fell in front of one of the trains that he so faithfully met. The monument overlooks the depot where he waited and watched for so many years.

SPRING BAKE

2 cups cubed, cooked ham
2 cups cooked rice
1 cup grated Old English cheese
1/2 cup canned milk (undiluted)
1 can cream of asparagus soup
2 tablespoons grated onion
3/4 cup cornflakes
3 tablespoons melted butter

Combine the first six ingredients in 2-quart lightly buttered baking dish. Sprinkle with cornflakes (slightly crushed) mixed with melted butter. Bake at 375 degrees for 20-30 minutes. Do not overbake. Garnish with hot buttered asparagus spears or parsley. Serves 4.

MAIN DISHES

Many farms across Montana raise pigs to ship to market or fill their own freezers. Pork is a table meat of various cuts and preparations and is 50 percent leaner than in previous years, making for healthier eating. It has been noted that most folks can't look at a pig, of any size, without smiling just a little bit.

PORK CHOP BAKE

4 lean pork chops
2 cups soft white bread cubes - using crust
1/2 cup chopped onion
3 tablespoons melted margarine
Water to moisten
Sage or thyme to taste
1 can cream of mushroom soup, diluted with 1/3 cup water

Brown pork chops. Put in single layer in baking dish. Mix bread, onion, margarine, seasonings, and water to moisten. Sprinkle over chops. Combine soup and the 1/3 cup water. Pour over all. Bake uncovered for 1 hour at 325 degrees or until pork chops are tender.

The abundant supply of subsurface coal near Colstrip has made this area one of the largest coal producers in the world. Strip mining is the process used where the surface rock is removed and the coal is dug out directly. Traveling across Montana, you will see trains loaded with coal. Each car holds about 100 tons.

PORK CHOP - APPLE KRAUT DINNER

"excellent chops dish"

4 pork chops or shoulder steaks
Salt and pepper
1 teaspoon caraway seeds
1/3 cup brown sugar
3 tablespoons chopped onion
1 can sauerkraut (medium)
2 apples

Brown chops in small amount of fat in dutch oven or electric skillet. Season with salt and pepper. Remove chops from pan and pour off fat. Add kraut, caraway seed, sugar, onions, and sliced apples; that have been mixed thoroughly. Top with chops. Cover and let cook at low heat for 1 hour or until meat is tender, basting chops with juices in pan.

MAIN DISHES

The Lewis and Clark expedition spent more time and covered more miles in Montana than any other area while searching for a possible water route by means of the Missouri and Columbia rivers to the Pacific Ocean.

SCHWEIZERSCHNITZEL ROLL-UPS

2 1/2 pounds veal cutlets (about 10)
2 1/2 cups (4 -1/2 ounce size cans) deviled ham
2 1/2 tablespoons chopped onion
1 8-ounce package cream cheese
2 beaten eggs
1 1/4 cups fine dry bread crumbs
5 tablespoons margarine or butter
3 envelopes dry mushroom gravy mix
3/4 cup dry sherry

With meat mallet, pound cutlets very thin. Mix deviled ham with onion; spread on cutlets just to the edge. Slice cream cheese into thin strips; place 3 strips on each slice of veal. Roll cutlets, fasten with picks. Dip in egg and then in crumbs. Brown veal on all sides in skillet. Transfer veal to a large casserole and remove picks.

Gravy: Pour the required amount of water into skillet, add gravy mix and sherry. Cook and stir until mixture is thick; pour over veal rolls. Bake covered at 350 degrees for 45-60 minutes or until veal is tender. Serves 8.

Montanans are outdoor people, enjoying their way of life.Traveling down Montana's highways and backroads, or parked in the local small towns on a Saturday, are "outfits"; meaning a pickup with a gun rack in the back window and one or two dogs enjoying the rough ride.

BREAKFAST CASSEROLE

"perfect for a weekend brunch"

Butter 9x13 inch pan.

1 layer white bread (crust removed)
1 layer chopped ham
1 layer little smokies (chopped)
1 layer chopped green onions
1 large can mushrooms
1 layer grated mild Cheddar cheese
1 dozen eggs, beaten until foamy
1 cup milk
Salt and pepper to taste

Layer first six ingredients in the buttered pan. Beat eggs until foamy, add milk, salt, and pepper. Pour egg mixture over all. Cover and let stand overnight. In the morning, bake at 350 degrees for one hour.

MAIN DISHES

Many Irish, as well as other ethnic groups, migrated to Butte in the 1880's to work the copper mines. To this day, many descendants still reside there. The city is noted for its St. Patrick's Day celebration when thousands of "leprechauns" trek to Butte for the festive day of green.

CORNED BEEF AND CABBAGE

"a bit of Irish"

5-6 pounds corned beef brisket
A few celery tops
2 onions, sliced
2 cloves of garlic
2 bay leaves
7 medium potatoes
6 or 7 carrots
Cabbage, sliced in wedges

Place brisket in large kettle with seasonings. Cover with cold water, bringing to boil. Reduce heat to simmer and cook for five hours or until beef is tender. Remove meat from liquid, wrap in foil to keep warm. Add vegetables and cover. Bring to boil and cook about 25-30 minutes. Slice meat thin and serve with vegetables.

Mountain ranges take up two-fifths of Montana's 147,138 square miles. The Beartooths, Missions, Cabinets, Highwoods, Bitterroots, and Crazies are just a few of the ranges where hunters go in hopes of bringing down an elk or deer.

BAKED ELK STEAK

"from the heart of elk country"

- **2 pounds elk steak**
- **1/2 clove of garlic**
- **1/4 cup flour, mixed with salt and pepper**
- **1 small bay leaf**
- **3 tablespoons oil**
- **1 6-ounce can tomato paste**
- **1 large onion, sliced**
- **1 1/2 cups water**
- **1/2 teaspoon salt**
- **Dash of pepper**
- **1/4 teaspoon thyme**
- **1/4 teaspoon sugar**
- **1 green pepper, cut into rings**

Cut steak into serving pieces. Rub with garlic, sprinkle with salt and pepper and pound flour into steak. Heat oil in large skillet, brown steak on both sides. Remove meat and place in casserole. Pour off oil from skillet. Mix tomato paste, water, and seasonings; heat in same skillet. Arrange onion and green pepper over meat. Pour tomato mixture over all. Cover tightly with lid or aluminum foil. Bake in preheated oven at 350 degrees for 1 1/2 to 2 hours, or until meat is fork tender.

Fall bird hunting is popular in Montana. Many hunters look forward with anticipation for the opening day, usually beginning around the middle of October. The recipe below is for those of you who are successful.

ELIZABETH M. STEELE'S BAKED PHEASANT

Two or three pheasants
Bread dressing
Salt pork or bacon strips

Remove pin feathers and singe dressed pheasants. Rinse well inside and out. Drain well.

Make bread dressing of onion, celery, salt, pepper, sage, and bread crumbs. Saute onion and celery in butter until yellow. Combine with bread and seasonings, adding a little milk so that it is moist. Pack dressing lightly into pheasant cavities (fill both neck and body cavities). Sew up if you wish. Place pork or bacon slices over breasts and legs of birds. Place birds on rack in roaster. Cover and roast at 350 degrees for about 2 hours, depending on size of pheasants. Remove from roaster when done and make gravy. Discard pork. Serve gravy separately over rice or potatoes.

SQUASH SPAGHETTINI ALLA SQUASH

(a recipe for spaghetti squash)

2 15-ounce cans tomato sauce
5 fresh basil leaves or 1 tablespoon dried leaf
1 tablespoon Worcestershire sauce
2 teaspoons powdered oregano or 1 tablespoon dried leaf
Dash of cayenne
1/2 teaspoon salt
1/2 teaspoon freshly ground pepper (white is preferred)
1/2 teaspoon paprika
1 tablespoon honey
2 medium to large Walla Walla sweet onions (or Bermudas)
1 medium zucchini squash and 1 large spaghetti squash
2 cloves garlic
2 tablespoons olive oil

Heat sauce in large sauce pan. Mince basil leaves and add them to sauce along with next 7 ingredients. Remember, fresh herbs are recommended for this dish. Cover and simmer very slowly for about an hour. Meanwhile, peel and split zucchini lengthwise and scoop out small seeds with a teaspoon; slice each half about 1/4 inch thick. Mince onion and garlic and saute with zucchini in olive oil until onions are clear. Add this mixture to simmering sauce and continue to simmer at least 30 minutes. While sauce bubbles, prepare spaghetti squash by halving, scooping out seeds, and boiling in large amount of water for about 30 minutes or bake halves like you would for pumpkin. Allow to cool a little for handling. Gently scoop out delicate, stringy squash onto serving plates and dot with butter. Ladle the sauce over the squash. This dish may be served topped with grated mozzarella and with garlic bread or whole wheat biscuits. Serves 4-6.

Sweet Treats

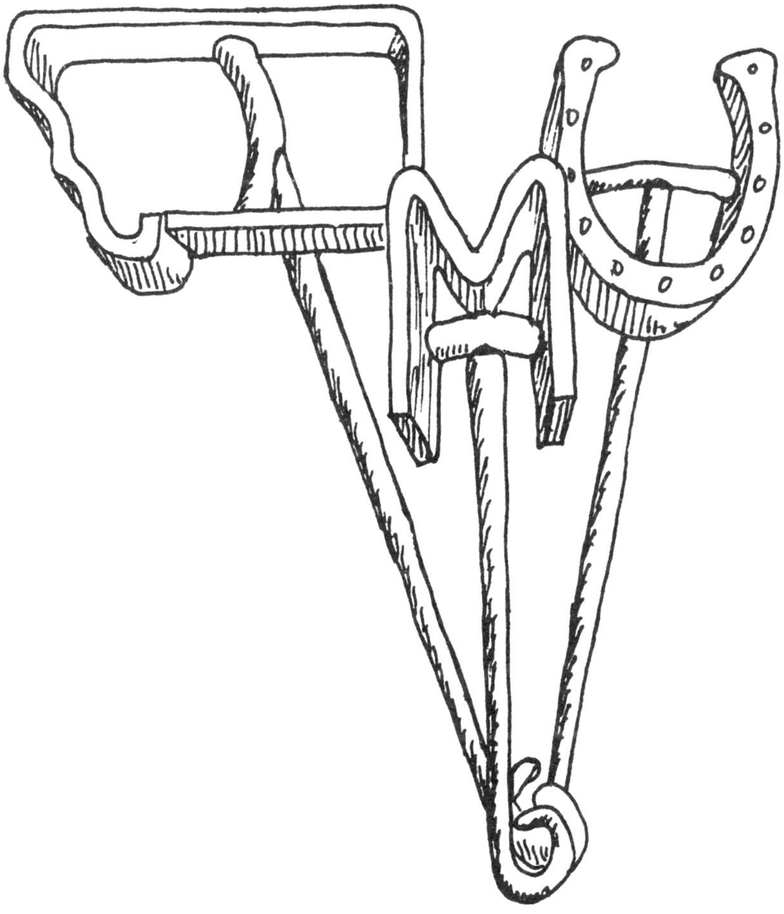

OATMEAL COOKIES

Taken from Home Cook, a handwritten Montana
Cookbook by early Montana ranch wives.
Most everyone cooked with wood stoves and there were no times, temperatures, or directions listed. They went mainly by taste and smell.

2 cups oats (uncooked)
2 cups flour
1 cup sugar
1 cup butter
2 eggs
4 tablespoons sweet milk, dissolve 1 scant teaspoon soda in milk
1 teaspoon vanilla
1 cup raisins
1 teaspoon baking powder

"Bake and eat but do not make yourself sick."

Spectacular sightings of bald eagles in Glacier National Park and along the Missouri River draw the interest of many Montana natives and tourists. Hundreds of eagles gather and feed on the spawning Kokanee salmon.

HELLO DOLLIES

Melt **1/2 cup butter or margarine** in 8x11 inch pan.

Add the following in order:
1 cup graham cracker crumbs
1 cup chopped nuts
1 cup chocolate chips
1 cup coconut

Pour **1 cup of Eagle Brand (sweetened condensed milk)** over top. Bake at 350 degrees for 20-25 minutes. Cool and cut in squares.

SWEET TREATS

Television first came to Montana on November 9, 1953 when KOOK-TV in Billings did the first broadcast beginning at 6:00 p.m. that evening. Area residents enjoyed their evening watching shows such as "The Red Buttons Show" and "Heroes of the Saddle."

OLD FASHIONED CHOCOLATE CHIP COOKIES

2/3 cup butter
1/2 cup white sugar
1/2 cup brown sugar (packed)
1 egg
1 teaspoon vanilla
1 cup flour
1/2 teaspoon baking soda
1/2 teaspoon salt
1/2 cup chopped nuts
1 cup (6-ounce package) chocolate chips

Mix butter, sugar, egg, and vanilla thoroughly. (Add 1/4 cup more flour if you prefer a softer cookie.) Stir the dry ingredients together and blend in the egg mixture. Mix in chopped nuts and chocolate chips. Drop cookies with a teaspoon on an ungreased cookie sheet. Bake at 350 degrees for 8 minutes or until lightly browned.

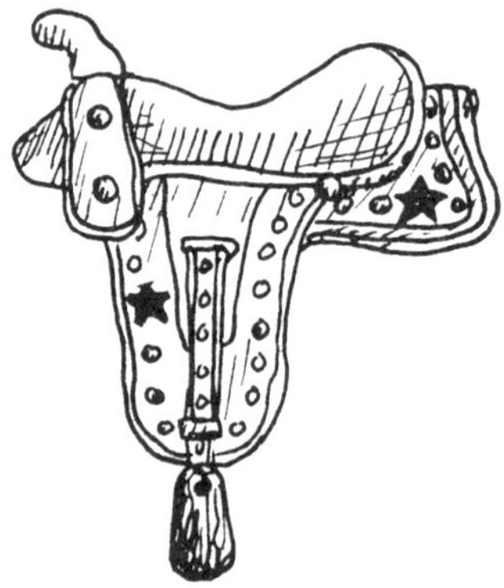

The state's first college was located in Deer Lodge, opening in 1878 as Montana Collegiate Institute. It received strong support but financial problems continued to rise. The college lost enrollment, closing once, reopening, and the final closing came in 1916.

FILLED CREAM CHEESE FOLDOVERS

2 sticks butter, softened
1 8-ounce package cream cheese, softened
2 1/2 cups flour
3/4 cups apricot or strawberry jam

Cream butter and cream cheese; add flour and mix well. Chill. Roll dough out thin and cut into 2-inch squares. Place 1/2 teaspoon jam in the center of the square. Fold the two opposite corners and pinch together in the center. Bake on an ungreased baking sheet for 10-12 minutes at 350 degrees.

GUMDROP COOKIES

1 cup shortening
1 cup brown sugar
1 cup white sugar
2 eggs
1 teaspoon vanilla
2 cups sifted flour
1 teaspoon baking powder
1/2 teaspoon baking soda
1/4 to 1/2 teaspoon salt
2 cups quick cooking oats
1 cup coconut
1 cup gumdrops, cut up (excluding licorice)

Thoroughly cream shortening and sugars. Add eggs and beat well. Sift dry ingredients and add to creamed mixture. Blend. Add oats, coconut, and gumdrops, and mix with spoon until blended. Roll dough into small balls. Place on greased cookie sheet. Press each ball with a fork. Bake at 350-375 degrees for about 10 minutes.

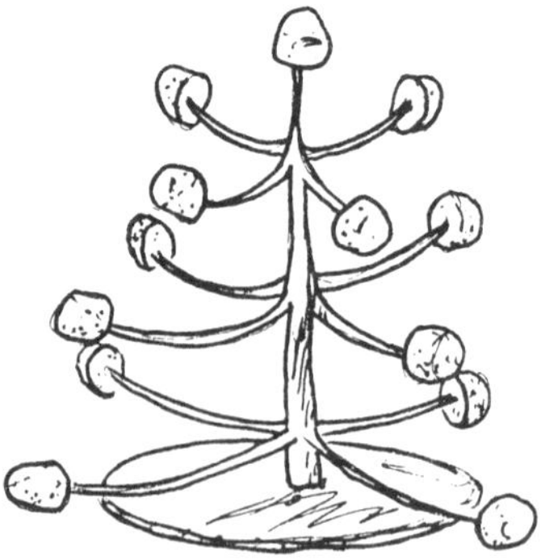

Bozeman is sometimes selected as the site for the Wally Byam Airstream Caravan Club. The Club is named after Wally Byam, the man who invented the Airstream travel trailer. The rally is then held in late June on the University campus surroundings. Between 7,000 to 8,000 Airstream trailer owners gather together for a fun filled week, coming from across the United States, Mexico, and Canada.

MONSTER COOKIES

"fun treats for little and big monsters"

12 eggs
1 pound butter
2 pounds brown sugar
4 cups white sugar
8 teaspoons baking powder
3 pounds peanut butter
18 cups oatmeal
1 pound M & M's
1 pound chocolate chips
1 tablespoon vanilla
1 tablespoon corn syrup

Mix in order given. Use 1/4 cup dough for each cookie. Put 6 cookies on lightly oiled pan. Press flat. Bake 15 minutes at 350 degrees.

In February, rules of the competition are posted as Helena gets ready for the annual Race to the Sky for sled dogs. The race covers 300 and 500 miles. Mushers come from all over the United States vying for the purse. Some are novices and some are past prize winners. The route winds over the Continental Divide with elevations over 7,000 feet. It has been noted that this dog sled race is the most challenging in the lower 48 states.

CORNFLAKE COOKIES

2 cups sifted flour
1 teaspoon baking soda
1/2 teaspoon salt
1/2 teaspoon baking powder
1 1/2 cups shortening
1 cup white sugar
1 cup brown sugar
2 eggs, well beaten
1 teaspoon vanilla
2 cups cornflakes
2 cups coconut

Sift first 4 ingredients together, (set aside). Cream shortening and sugar. Add eggs and vanilla, then add first ingredients. Lastly add coconut and cornflakes. Drop by teaspoon on lightly oiled cookie sheet. Bake at 350 degrees for 8-10 minutes or until light brown.

Fort Peck Dam, located on the Missouri River, is one of the largest hydraulically earth-filled dams in the world. Many Montanans still recall the memories of the building of the dam during the 1930's. It was known as "Our Dam" and President Franklin D. Roosevelt visited the construction site twice. It employed over 10,000 workers and took over six years to complete.

RODNEY'S SUGAR COOKIES

1 cup shortening
1/2 cup brown sugar
1/2 cup white sugar
1 egg, beaten
1 teaspoon vanilla
2 cups flour
1/2 teaspoon salt
2 teaspoons cream of tartar
1 teaspoon baking soda

Cream shortening and sugars, add egg and remaining ingredients. Mix well. Roll into small balls, flatten with glass dipped in sugar. Place a half walnut on each if desired or use a glass with a design on the bottom. Bake for about 10 minutes at 350 degrees.

On August 17, 1959, one of the most severe earthquakes ever recorded in the United States occurred a few miles northwest of West Yellowstone. Quake Lake was formed when part of a mountain toppled into the Madison River. Twenty-eight campers lost their lives that night as they were sleeping in a campground at the base of the mountain. The quake measured 7.1 on the Richter Scale.

GINGER COOKIES

"a large batch for a large crowd"

2 2/3 cups butter or margarine
5 cups sugar
5 eggs
1 1/2 cups molasses
10 cups flour
10 teaspoons baking soda
5 teaspoons salt
4 1/2 tablespoons ginger
5 teaspoons cinnamon

Cream butter, eggs, and sugar. Add molasses. Mix dry ingredients together. Add to the creamed mixture, mixing well. Roll dough in 1-inch balls and dip in additional sugar. Place balls on greased cookie sheets and bake for about 10 minutes at 350 degrees. Yield: 160 cookies.

The Missouri River Float is probably one of the most gratifying ways to enjoy the last bit of untouched wilderness on the "Mighty Mo". Many enthusiasts put their canoes or boats in at Fort Benton and float to the Fred Robinson Bridge, south of Malta. Floaters camp and fish along the gentle 149 mile trip.

MRS. ROBINSON'S OATMEAL THINS

Mix together:
1/2 cup flour
1 1/2 cups oatmeal
1/4 cup white sugar
1/2 teaspoon baking soda

Melt together:
1/2 cup butter
1 tablespoon real maple syrup

Stir together first and second mixtures. Drop by small amounts onto ungreased cookie sheet. Bake at 375 degrees for 7-8 minutes. Let cool slightly before removing from pan.

"TO MY VALENTINE" OATMEAL COOKIES

2 1/2 cups sifted flour
1 teaspoon baking powder
1/2 teaspoon salt
3/4 cup butter or margarine, softened
3/4 cup sugar
2 tablespoons milk
1 egg
1 teaspoon vanilla
1 cup oatmeal, quick or long cook

Sift flour, baking powder, and salt into bowl. Add butter, sugar, milk, egg, and vanilla. Beat until well blended, about 2 minutes. Stir in oats. Roll out on lightly floured board or canvas to 1/4 inch thickness. Cut with heart shaped cookie cutter. Bake on greased sheet in 350 degree oven for about 10-12 minutes. Frost and decorate.

Frosting:
1/2 stick butter, softened
2 cups powdered sugar
1 tablespoon maraschino cherry juice
2 tablespoons milk or cream
3/4 teaspoon vanilla or almond flavoring

Cream together butter and powdered sugar; add cherry juice, milk and vanilla. Mix well.

Giant Springs, located on the northeast side of Great Falls, is one of the largest fresh water springs in the world. It pumps 388,800,000 gallons of water every 24 hours year around, at a constant temperature of 52 degrees. It was discovered by the Lewis and Clark Expedition in 1805.

EASY FILLED COOKIES

1 cup soft shortening
2 cups brown sugar (packed)
2 eggs
1/2 cup water or buttermilk
1 teaspoon vanilla
3 1/2 cups sifted flour
1/2 teaspoon salt
1 teaspoon baking soda
1/8 teaspoon cinnamon

Mix thoroughly; shortening, brown sugar, and eggs. Stir in vanilla and water. Sift together and stir in flour, salt, soda, and cinnamon. Drop with teaspoon on ungreased baking sheet. Place 1/2 teaspoon date filling on dough; cover with another 1/2 teaspoon dough. Bake at 375 degrees for 8-10 minutes.

Filling:
2 cups dates, cut fine
3/4 cup sugar
3/4 cup water
1/2 cup chopped nuts

Cook together slowly; dates, sugar, and water, stirring constantly until thickened. Add nuts. Cool.

West Yellowstone is one of the three Montana entrances to Yellowstone Park. It is an enjoyable place to be in summer or winter as it has captured the title "Snowmobile Capital of the World". Except for a couple main streets, all streets are open to "sled traffic".

SUGAR COOKIES

2 cups white sugar
1 cup butter
3 eggs, well beaten
2 teaspoons vanilla
6 1/2 cups flour, sifted
2 teaspoons baking powder
1 teaspoon baking soda
1 teaspoon salt
1 cup sour cream

Mix butter, sugar, eggs, and vanilla. Measure flour and blend together all dry ingredients. Add to creamed mixture alternately with the sour cream. Chill dough before rolling. Roll thin on pastry cloth and cut with 2-inch cutter. Place on greased baking sheet. Sprinkle with sugar if desired. Bake 7 to 9 minutes at 350 degrees.

The State Orphanage was located in Twin Bridges. It housed some 5,000 children throughout the years before its final closure in 1975.

AUNT SALLY'S COCOA DROPS

1/2 cup butter or margarine
1 cup sugar
1 egg
3/4 cup buttermilk or sour milk
1 teaspoon vanilla
1 3/4 cups flour
1/2 teaspoon baking soda
1/2 teaspoon salt
1/2 cup cocoa
1 cup chopped nuts

Mix butter, sugar, and egg thoroughly. Stir in buttermilk and vanilla. Sift the dry ingredients and add to mixture. Stir in nuts. Chill 1 hour. Drop by teaspoon unto lightly greased cookie sheet (about 2 inches apart). Bake for 8 to 10 minutes at 375 degrees. Cool and frost with a chocolate frosting.

SWEET TREATS

The Going-To-The-Sun Road opened across Glacier National Park on July 11, 1933. The work took 12 years to complete as workmen chiseled in solid rock and dangled on ropes 1,000 feet above the narrow passages. Supplies were brought in by horses. The Road spans over fifty miles and links the Park from east to west.

CARROT COOKIES

3/4 cup shortening
3/4 cup white sugar
1 beaten egg
1 cup cooked carrots (mashed)
2 cups flour
2 teaspoons baking powder
1/4 teaspoon salt
1 teaspoon vanilla
1/3 cup chopped nuts

Cream shortening and sugar, add egg and carrots. Mix well. Add dry ingredients and stir in vanilla and nuts. Drop on lightly greased cookie sheet. Bake at 375 degrees for 12-15 minutes. Cool and frost with orange frosting.

Orange Frosting:
3 tablespoons melted butter
Juice and rind of one orange
1 cup powdered sugar

Stir ingredients together and frost cooled cookies.

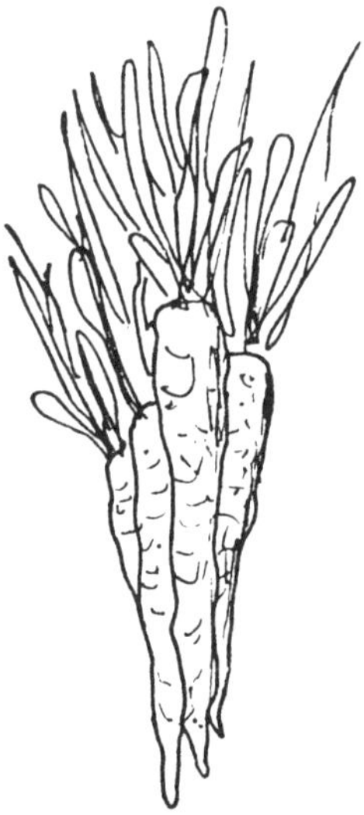

Governor Sidney Edgerton appointed Thomas J. Dimsdale to be the first territorial superintendent of schools of Montana in 1866. Dimsdale was also editor of Montana's first newspaper, The Post and author of the book, The Vigilantes of Montana, which was the first book published in the state. Mr. Dimsdale was a well qualified man indeed.

MELTAWAY SHORTBREAD

1/2 cup butter
1/2 cup vegetable shortening
3 tablespoons sugar
2 cups sifted flour
1 cup flaked coconut (angel-type)

Cream together all ingredients. Roll into 2 rolls, wrap in wax paper and chill well. Slice and bake on ungreased cookie sheet at 375 degrees until a very light brown. Do not overcook. Dip in powdered sugar.

Kid Curry, Butch Cassidy, and the Sundance Kid were identified as among the bandits that robbed the Great Northern No. 3 passenger train in broad daylight on July 3, 1901 west of Malta. They dynamited the express car safe and escaped with $41,000 in unsigned bank notes.

CARAMEL BROWNIES

1 14-ounce bag of light caramels
1 small can evaporated milk
1 devils food cake mix
3/4 cup margarine, melted
1 6-ounce package chocolate chips

Melt caramels in 1/3 cup evaporated milk. Cover after melted. Mix cake mix, 1/3 cup evaporated milk, and melted margarine together. Put 1/2 of batter in 9x13 inch prepared cake pan. Bake for 6 minutes at 350 degrees. Cool on rack for 2 minutes. Spread caramel mixture over baked cake. Sprinkle with chocolate chips. Put remaining cake batter on top of caramel and chocolate chips. Bake for 15-18 minutes. Brownies will be soft.

Eureka, a town way up in the northwest corner of the state, has been growing some of the finest Christmas trees in the nation. It is sometimes called "Montana's Christmas Tree Paradise" and the market for these trees has become nationwide.

CAKE BROWNIES

2 cups sugar
1/2 cup butter or margarine
4 slightly beaten eggs
2 squares melted chocolate
1/2 cup sweet milk
1 1/2 cups cake flour
1/2 teaspoon salt
1 teaspoon vanilla
1 cup nutmeats, optional

Cream sugar and butter. Add beaten eggs and melted chocolate. Add milk, flour, and salt, alternately. Add vanilla and nuts. Pour into 9x9 inch greased and floured pan. Bake 30 minutes at 350 degrees.

FUDGE FROSTING

2 1-ounce squares unsweetened chocolate
3 cups sugar
3 tablespoons light corn syrup
1/4 teaspoon salt
1 cup milk
1/4 cup butter or margarine
1 teaspoon vanilla

Butter sides of heavy 3-quart saucepan. In it, combine first 5 ingredients. Cook and stir over low heat until sugar dissolves and chocolate melts. Cook to soft ball stage (234 degrees) without stirring. Remove from heat; add butter and cool to warm (110 degrees) without stirring. Add vanilla; beat until mixture is of spreading consistency.

Hundreds of Montana churches were established with the help of Rev. William Wesley Van Orsdel, who was born on March 20, 1848. From 1872 to 1919, "Brother Van" covered the state, making friends everywhere he went while preaching The Word. He most often went to the local saloons where he would ask the owner to close the bar so he could hold services. The communities were enthused about his visits and would come from miles around to hear him. "Brother Van" preached his last sermon in Malta. He suffered a stroke on October 8, 1919 and died on December 19. He was buried in Helena on Christmas Eve with the flags at the Capitol flying half-mast.

BERLINER KRANSER

"special for the holiday season"

2 cups butter (do not substitute)
1 cup sugar
4 yolks of hard boiled eggs
4 cups flour
4 yolks of 4 raw eggs
Drop of almond
Save egg whites for dipping wreaths

Powder the yolk of hard boiled eggs, mix in yolk of raw eggs and when smooth, add sugar gradually. Add flavoring, then knead and alternate with butter and flour. Break dough in pieces the size of a walnut, roll and shape into small wreaths. Dip in egg whites and sprinkle with ground nuts. Bake in preheated oven at 325 degrees for 18 to 20 minutes.

SWEET TREATS

Charles M. Russell, one of Montana's famous cowboy artists, was born in Missouri in 1864 and came to Montana as a young boy. In his early days, he worked as a cowboy around Judith Basin County and painted in his spare time. Realizing his abilities, he soon traded his nite hawkin' for a palette and his popularity began to grow. The art critics say Russell's most famous painting is hanging in the Capitol Building in Helena. It is twenty-five feet long and twelve feet high and portrays the meeting of Lewis and Clark with the Flathead Indians.

DANISH BUTTER SANDWICHES

"deilig"

1 cup butter
3/4 cup brown sugar
1 egg yolk
2 1/4 cups flour

Cream butter and brown sugar together, add egg yolk and beat to mix. Gradually add flour, beating until mixture holds together. Roll dough into small balls, place on cookie sheet and dip fork in flour and press indentations one way. Bake at 325 degrees for 15-20 minutes. Cool. Match up two cookies and put 1 teaspoon of filling between.

BROWN BUTTER FILLING

2 tablespoons butter
1/2 teaspoon vanilla
1 1/4 cups powdered sugar
6 tablespoons evaporated milk

Brown butter in heavy saucepan and add remaining ingredients. Stir until smooth.

Tart, red rhubarb grows well in Montana gardens in late spring and early summer. Montana cooks make rhubarb cobbler, rhubarb pie, rhubarb sauce, and rhubarb cake in their attempt to keep up with the bountiful crop. The following is a layered cookie bar for that morning coffee break.

RHUBARB BARS

2 tablespoons cornstarch
1/4 cup water
3 cups rhubarb, cut fine
1 1/2 cups sugar
1 teaspoon vanilla

Crust:
1 1/2 cups oatmeal, uncooked
1 1/2 cups flour
1 cup brown sugar
1/2 teaspoon baking soda
1/2 teaspoon salt
1 cup margarine
1/2 cup chopped nuts (optional)

In saucepan, dissolve cornstarch in water. Add rhubarb, sugar, and vanilla. Cook until thickened. Stir together flour, oats, brown sugar, soda, and salt. Cut in margarine as for pie crust. If desired, toss lightly with nuts. Pat one half mixture into 9x13 inch pan. Spread rhubarb mixture over crust. Sprinkle with remaining crumbs and bake at 350 degrees for 30-35 minutes. Refrigerate several hours before cutting.

Yellowstone National Park is the oldest and largest park in the lower 48 states. It is often called "nature's wonderland" with its spouting geysers, mountains, canyons, streams, radiant pools, lakes, and waterfalls. Montana holds the honor of having three of the park's entrances; West Yellowstone, Gardiner, and Silver Gate.

MOTHER FORD'S OATMEAL COOKIES

3/4 cup shortening
1 cup sugar
2 eggs
4 tablespoons sweet milk
3/4 teaspoon baking soda
2 teaspoons cinnamon
1/2 teaspoon salt
2 cups flour
2 cups dry rolled oats (regular)
1 cup chopped raisins

Cream shortening and sugar and add eggs and milk. Mix until well blended. Add dry ingredients, adding raisins last. Mix well. Drop by rounded teaspoon onto greased cookie sheet and bake for 10-12 minutes at 350 degrees.

The Stillwater Mining Company, located several miles south of Nye, is mining platinum and palladium. The metals are used for automotive electronics and jewelry. These two metals are mined on a large scale at only two other places in the world, South Africa and Russia.

APPLE BARS

2 1/2 cups flour
1 teaspoon salt
1 cup shortening
1 egg yolk/milk
2 handfuls crushed cornflakes
8 to 10 cooking apples
1 cup sugar
1 teaspoon cinnamon
Egg white

Add enough milk to make 2/3 cup with the egg yolk. Combine egg yolk mixture, flour, salt, and shortening and mix as you would for a pie crust. Roll 1/2 dough to fit 10 1/2 x 15 1/2" cookie tray. Sprinkle bottom crust with two handfuls of crushed cornflakes. Peel apples and slice and arrange over pie crust. Sprinkle with sugar and cinnamon. Roll out other half of crust, put on top, pinch edges. Beat egg white until stiff. Brush over top. Bake for 1 hour at 400 degrees. Frost bars while warm, combining **1 cup powdered sugar, 1 tablespoon water**, and **1 teaspoon vanilla.** Cut into bars.

Montana has several state parks including the Medicine Rock State Park located near Ekalaka. The Medicine Rocks cover several miles. They stand stately, displaying many various formations. Theodore Roosevelt visited the area in 1883, saying how "fantastically beautiful" they were.

LEMON BARS

1 cup butter
2 cups sifted flour
1/2 cup powdered sugar
Pinch of salt
4 eggs, beaten
2 cups sugar
3 tablespoons flour
1 teaspoon baking powder
4 tablespoons lemon juice
Grated lemon rind

Combine the first four ingredients, mixing until smooth, then press into a 9x13 inch greased pan. Bake at 350 degrees for 15-20 minutes, but do not brown. While crust is baking, prepare topping by combining last six ingredients. Pour over bottom crust and bake 20-25 minutes at 350 degrees. Sift powdered sugar over top while still warm; cut into squares. Cool before removing from pan.

On March 5, 1862, George P. White and widow Mrs. Joseph Minsinger were married and this wedding is believed to be the first marriage of two white people in Montana.

SPICE COOKIE BARS

1 cup raisins
1 cup water
1/2 cup salad oil
1 cup sugar
1 slightly beaten egg
1 3/4 cups sifted flour
1 teaspoon nutmeg
1 teaspoon cinnamon
1 teaspoon allspice
1/2 teaspoon cloves
1/4 teaspoon salt
1 teaspoon baking soda
1/2 cup chopped nuts

Combine raisins and water. Bring to a boil, remove from heat. Stir in oil, cool to lukewarm. Stir in sugar, then egg. Sift together dry ingredients and mix into raisin mixture. Stir in nuts. Pour into well greased 9x13 inch pan. Bake at 375 degrees, about 20 minutes or until a toothpick comes out clean. While still warm, sprinkle with powdered sugar or serve with a warm vanilla sauce.

REESE'S PEANUT BUTTER BARS

1 1/2 packages graham crackers, crushed fine
1 3/4 cups powdered sugar
1/2 cup melted butter or margarine
1 1/2 cups peanut butter
1 teaspoon vanilla
1/2 cup crushed dry roasted peanuts (optional)

Mix together and spread in 9x13 inch pan. Do not bake.

Icing:
1/4 cup butter
1/3 cup milk
1 cup sugar

Boil above ingredients together for one minute.

Add to icing mixture:
1/2 cup chocolate chips
5 large marshmallows

Stir until dissolved. Cool and frost bars. Cut into small squares. Keep in refrigerator.

Homes in Helena and Butte were the first to enjoy electric lights, in August and November of 1882. Billings was the first city with hydroelectric power coming about in 1887. Back then, Billings had one streetlight for every block in the business district and on every other block in the residential area.

PECAN BARS

Crust:
2 cups flour
1 cup brown sugar
1/2 cup shortening
1/2 cup butter
1 teaspoon salt
1 egg yolk
1 teaspoon vanilla

Filling:
4 eggs
3/4 cup sugar
1/2 cup butter
2 cups chopped pecans
1 1/4 cups dark syrup
1/2 cup flour
1 teaspoon vanilla

Combine crust ingredients and blend well. Press evenly into ungreased 10x15 inch pan. Bake at 350 degrees 12-15 minutes or until golden brown. For filling, combine eggs and sugar. Stir in syrup and butter. Blend well. Add flour, vanilla, and pecans. Pour over warm crust. Bake at 350 degrees for 15-20 minutes until set and golden brown. Cool and cut.

Dude ranches are popular vacation sites in Montana. You get treated as a "real ranch hand." Horseback riding, cookouts, and taking in some of Big Sky's other outdoor life are just a few of the adventures.

MONTANA RANCH ROMANCES

1/2 cup butter
1 cup flour
2 tablespoons sugar
1 1/2 cups brown sugar
2 eggs
1 teaspoon baking powder
1 cup coconut
1 teaspoon vanilla
1/2 cup walnuts

Cream first three ingredients, pack in greased 8x8 inch pan. Bake for 20 minutes at 325 degrees. In bowl, mix brown sugar, eggs, and baking powder. Add the last three ingredients to this mixture then spread on baked crust (first mixture). Bake for 30 to 35 minutes at 325 degrees or until meringue is nicely browned. (Use toothpick test.)

The official seal of Montana bears the motto "Oro-Y-Plata", the Spanish words for gold and silver. The central part of the seal includes a plow and a miner's pick and shovel with the Great Falls of the Missouri on the right and mountain scenery on the left. The seal was adopted on March 2, 1893.

BUTTER TARTS

Pie dough for double crust pie. Roll out and use wide mouth jar lid to cut. Place in approximate 2-inch tart tins that have been placed on cookie sheets.

1 cup currants
1 cup brown sugar
2 tablespoons butter
1 egg, beaten
1/2 teaspoon vanilla

Scald currants with 1 cup boiling water. Drain and while currants are still warm, add brown sugar, butter, and beaten egg. Stir well and add vanilla. Spoon into unbaked tart shells. Bake at 400 degrees for about 10 minutes - then set the oven at 350 degrees for another 10-15 minutes. Be careful not to overbake.

SANDBAKKELSE
(Scandinavian Sand Tarts)

Quantity: 8 to 10 dozen depending on how thin they are pressed into tins.

2 cups (one pound) unsalted butter
2 eggs, beaten
2 cups powdered sugar
1/2 teaspoon cardamon
4 cups flour

Mix in order given and chill dough in refrigerator. Press dough into sandbakkelse tins, placing a small ball of dough in the center of each tin. With the thumb, press dough evenly on inside of tin. Bake at 350 degrees for about 10-12 minutes or until golden brown.

Variation: You may substitute **1 teaspoon of almond extract or vanilla extract** in place of the cardamon, if you prefer.

These pastries are usually served without any filling but are delicious if filled with whipped cream or a nut filling.

PECAN SANDBAKKELSE FILLING

Bring to boil: **1/2 cup butter or margarine**
1/3 cup dark corn syrup
1 cup powdered sugar

Stir in **1 cup of chopped pecans.** Spoon mixture into baked sandbakkelse shells. Top with pecan halves, if desired. Bake at 350 degrees for about 5 minutes. Filling will fill about 4 dozen tarts.

Montana was admitted to the Union on November 8, 1889. It is the nation's fourth largest state, averaging 550 miles long and 275 miles wide. To the east lie the Great Plains. The Rocky Mountains cover the western part of the state. The Continental Divide runs north and south through most of the western section.

NUT CAKES

"a special Christmas treat"

1/2 cup butter
1 (3 ounce) package cream cheese
1 cup flour
1/2 teaspoon salt

Mix all together as for a pie crust. Make 24 balls and press into small muffin tins.

Filling
1 beaten egg
3/4 cup brown sugar
1 tablespoon melted butter
Pinch of salt
1/4 teaspoon vanilla
1/2 cup chopped nuts

Mix all ingredients except for nuts. Sprinkle small amount of nuts into each cup, then a teaspoon of the filling. Sprinkle rest of nuts on top. Bake at 350 degrees for 15 minutes, then bake an extra 10 minutes at 250 degrees.

The Great Falls Tribune sponsored Montana's first licensed radio station, KDYS, which began broadcasting in 1922. After 18 months, it went off the air and Montana's first permanent station was KFBB, which F.A. Buttrey began at Havre. The station later moved to Great Falls.

DIRT DESSERT

15 Oreo cookies (regular)
1/4 cup butter
1 quart vanilla ice cream
1/2 jar fudge topping
6 ounces whipped topping

Remove filling from Oreos. Using rolling pin, crush Oreos, making crumbs. Mix melted butter and cookie crumbs. Press into 9x9 inch pan. Add sliced ice cream. Pour fudge topping over ice cream. Spread on whipped topping. Crush more Oreos and sprinkle on top. Freeze. Cut into squares.

ELAINE'S SALTED NUT BARS

3 cups flour
1 1/2 cups brown sugar, packed
1 teaspoon salt
1 cup butter, softened (no substitute)
2 cups mixed nuts
1/2 cup light corn syrup
2 tablespoons butter
1 tablespoon water
1 6-ounce package butterscotch chips

In bowl: Combine flour, brown sugar, salt, and butter; blend well. Press into 10x15 inch ungreased jelly roll pan and bake in 350 degree oven for 10-12 minutes. Remove from oven and sprinkle mixed nuts over partially baked crust. In small saucepan, combine corn syrup, butter, water, and butterscotch chips. Boil 2 minutes, stirring constantly. Pour cooked mixture over nuts. Return to oven and bake 10-12 minutes or until golden brown. Cool completely before cutting.

Montana is a word derived from the Latin word meaning "mountainous." Granite Peak is the highest point in Montana at 12,799 feet, and is located in the Beartooths, south of Billings. The lowest point is 1,820 feet on the Kootenai River at the Montana-Idaho line.

FROZEN ORANGE DESSERT

Juice of 3 fresh oranges
Juice of 1 lemon
Add: **1/2 cup granulated sugar** and stir until dissolved. Pour in bottom of freezer tray or small pan and freeze.

When frozen: Whip **1/2 pint cream** and fold in **2/3 cup powdered sugar**. Spoon over frozen orange mixture and cover the top generously with **salted cashews**.

Montana has received world acclaim for its 4,000 miles of fishing streams that run north and south, east and west, and kiddie korner throughout the Big Sky. These streams are home to several different species of fish, including trout, walleye, northern pike, and the intriguing paddlefish.

STRAWBERRY DELIGHT

"summer dessert"

1/2 cup butter
1/4 cup brown sugar
1 cup flour
1/2 cup nuts, chopped
1 10-ounce package frozen strawberries
2 egg whites
1 cup sugar
1 teaspoon lemon juice
1 teaspoon vanilla
1/2 pint whipping cream

Cut butter into chunks. Put in 9x13 inch pan along with flour, sugar and nuts. Bake at 400 degrees for 15 minutes, stirring every few minutes to form crumbly mixture. Take out of oven and set a little less than 1/2 of crumbs aside. Press remaining crumbs into pan. Put strawberries, egg whites, sugar, lemon juice, and vanilla in large bowl and beat 20 minutes; scraping bowl occasionally. Whip cream and fold in. Pour over crust and sprinkle with remaining crumbs. Freeze. Cut in squares when ready to serve.

Small towns all across Montana hold Octoberfests. Booths with all sorts of saleable Montana-Made crafts are set up. Events are scheduled, such as sack races, watermelon eating contests, and tug of war. Various kinds of foods are available plus plenty of apple cider for everyone that attends. This seems to be a way of celebrating after harvest and getting ready for the long winter months ahead.

PUMPKIN SPICE DESSERT

First Step:
1 cup biscuit mix
1/2 cup quick oats
1/2 cup brown sugar
1/4 cup firm margarine

Mix until crumbly, press in 9x13 inch pan. Bake 10 minutes at 350 degrees, cool.

Second Step:
1 16-ounce can pumpkin
1 can evaporated milk (12 ounce)
2 eggs
3/4 cup sugar
1/2 teaspoon salt
1 teaspoon cinnamon
1/2 teaspoon ginger
1/4 teaspoon cloves

Beat ingredients with a mixer and pour over baked crust. Bake 20 minutes at 350 degrees.

Third Step:
3/4 cup chopped nuts
1/2 cup brown sugar
2 tablespoons firm margarine

Mix and sprinkle over top of partially baked pumpkin. Continue baking until set, approximately 15-20 minutes. Cool completely and serve with spiced whipped cream.

Fourth Step: Spiced Whipped Cream
1 cup whipping cream
1 teaspoon grated orange rind
1 tablespoon sugar
1/2 teaspoon cinnamon

Whip cream, gradually add sugar. Fold in orange rind and cinnamon.

The Museum of the Rockies opened in Bozeman in 1957 and has since expanded to three times its original size. The popular place is probably best known for its world class dinosaur collection.

DORTHEA'S BANANA SPLIT DESSERT

2 cups graham cracker crumbs
1 stick melted margarine
2 cups powdered sugar
2 8-ounce packages softened cream cheese
1 can crushed, drained pineapple
4 to 5 sliced bananas
1 large container whipped topping
Chopped nuts for topping

Mix crumbs and margarine, press into 9x13 inch pan. Beat powdered sugar and cream cheese two minutes and pour over crust. Layer pineapple and bananas. Top with whipped topping. Sprinkle with nuts and refrigerate.

SWEET TREATS

Virginia City is the site of the richest placer gold discovery ever made and former territorial capital. The town has been restored to relate back to the "Boom Days". The Virginia City Players, specializing in 19th Century entertainment, help relive some of that wild-west past by performing in the summer months.

BLUEBERRY SOUR CREAM DESSERT

1 package white cake mix
1/2 cup chopped nuts
1/2 cup graham cracker crumbs
1/2 cup melted butter
1 can blueberry pie filling (20 ounce)
1 cup sour cream
1 egg
1/4 teaspoon nutmeg

Combine cake mix, graham crackers, nuts, and butter at low speed until crumbly. Remove 1 1/2 cups for topping. Press remaining mixture into a 9 inch square pan. Spread with pie filling. In a small bowl, blend sour cream, egg, and nutmeg. Pour over pie filling. Sprinkle with reserved crumbs. Bake at 350 degrees for 40-45 minutes or until topping is golden. Serve warm or cold.

DANISH BREAKFAST DELIGHT
"good anytime"

2 cups sugar
4 eggs
1/2 teaspoon salt
4 cups flour
1 cup margarine
1 1/2 teaspoons baking powder
1 teaspoon vanilla
1 quart pie filling

Mix together margarine, sugar, and eggs. Gradually add dry ingredients. Spread three-fourths of batter in bottom of greased jelly roll pan. Spread pie filling on top. Dab on remaining batter. Bake at 350 degrees for 40-50 minutes. Cool and glaze.

Glaze:
3 tablespoons sugar
3 tablespoons milk
3 tablespoons margarine
1 teaspoon vanilla
Powdered sugar

Mix sugar, milk, and margarine in small pan. Heat thoroughly. Add enough powdered sugar to make the glaze. Add vanilla and drizzle over top.

Pow Wow celebrations are held throughout Montana Indian Reservations during the summer months. They feature Indian dance and drum displays and many arts and crafts. The Pow Wows usually begin with a grand parade of dancers in colorful costumes. The Museum of Northern Plains Indians is located in Browning, where you can learn the background of the Native American culture and tradition.

CHERRIES IN THE SNOW

1 cup milk
1 cup powdered sugar
1 (12 ounce) dairy whipped topping
2 8-ounce packages cream cheese
1 angel food cake, homemade or bakery
1 can cherry pie filling

Mix the first 4 ingredients; fold in angel food that has been cut into cubes. Pour into 9x13 inch pan and refrigerate. Just before serving, pour cherry pie filling over top and spread evenly.

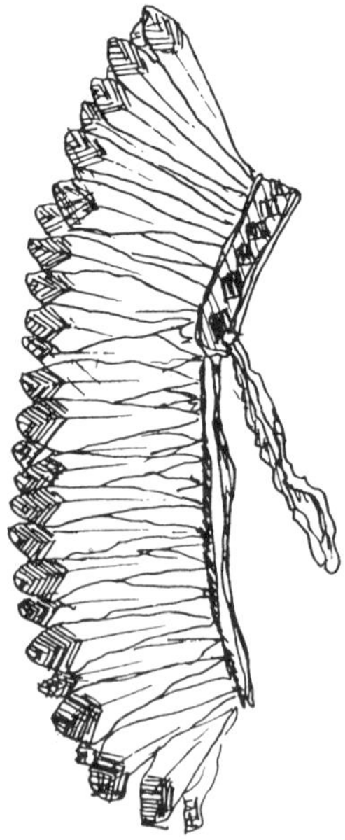

Huckleberry patches in western Montana are popular places in late summer and early fall. The berries are blue-black in color and have a sharp taste. They are delicious in hot cakes, pies, and other special desserts.

HUCKLEBERRY CHEESECAKE

1 9-inch graham cracker pie crust (unbaked)
1 12-ounce package cream cheese, softened
2 eggs
1/2 cup white sugar
1 teaspoon vanilla
2 cups huckleberries
1/2 cup sugar (for berries)
1 1/2 teaspoons cornstarch
1/4 cup lemon juice

Beat together cheese, eggs, 1/2 cup sugar, and vanilla until fluffy. Pour into pie crust and bake at 350 degrees for 20 minutes. Cool. Simmer berries with sugar and lemon juice in pan for five minutes. Thicken with cornstarch. Pour over cheesecake. Chill overnight. Makes one 9-inch pie.

Canyon Ferry, Hebgen, Flathead, and Georgetown Lakes are just a few of Montana's larger bodies of water that provide excellent fishing. Rainbow trout, perch, brown trout, and whitefish are the catches of the day.

LINDA'S DELICIOUS CHEESECAKE

Crust:
3/4 cup package Zwieback Toast
1/4 cup sugar
1/2 cup melted butter
1 teaspoon cinnamon

Roll toast into crumbs and mix ingredients. Press 3/4 of mixture on bottom and sides of a 10 inch spring form pan.

Cheese Filling:
2 pounds cream cheese
1 cup sugar
4 eggs, well beaten
1 tablespoon lemon juice

Beat eggs and one cup sugar until lemon colored; add cheese and lemon juice. Beat well with rotary beater. Pour into crust lined spring form pan. Bake in a 375 degree oven for 20 minutes.

Topping:
1 pint sour cream
4 tablespoons sugar
1 teaspoon vanilla

Blend sour cream, 4 tablespoons sugar and vanilla. Spread over partially baked cake. Sprinkle with remaining Zwieback crumbs, and bake in 475 degree oven for 10 minutes. Place in refrigerator for several hours. Remove one hour before serving.

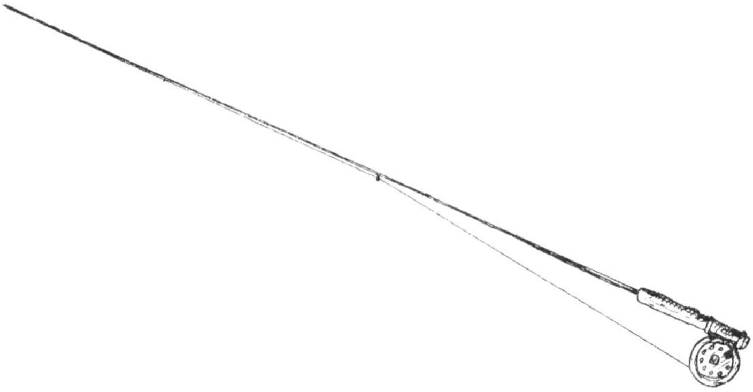

Nearly 95% of Montana's voters went to the polls in 1894 to select Helena or Anaconda, the two final contenders, for the permanent state capital race. Two of Montana's richest men, Marcus A. Daly, supporting Anaconda and William A. Clark, who was loyal to Helena, came forward and a fierce mud-slinging campaign for the capital began. Helena won by nearly 2,000 votes and the official celebration was on November 12, 1894. Businesses closed for the day and the city was decorated. Bands and fireworks contributed to the festivities. Nearly 15,000 people gathered at Last Chance Gulch to listen to Clark's victory speech.

CARROT CAKE

"the best"

4 eggs
1 1/2 cups sugar
1 1/2 cups vegetable oil
2 cups flour
2 teaspoons cinnamon
2 teaspoons baking powder
2 teaspoons baking soda
1 teaspoon salt
3 cups carrots (grated)
1 cup walnuts, chopped

Frosting:
Cream together:
1 8-ounce package cream cheese, softened
1/2 cup butter, softened
1 pound powdered sugar
Blend in:
1 cup very well drained crushed pineapple
1 teaspoon vanilla

In large bowl, beat eggs until frothy, then beat in sugar a little at a time. Beat mixture until lemon colored and light. Beat in vegetable oil, gradually. Sift together the dry ingredients. Fold mixture into egg mixture, a little at a time. Fold in carrots and nuts and combine well. Pour into 3 well-greased and floured 8 inch round cake pans and bake at 350 degrees in preheated oven for 30-35 minutes. Let layers cool in pans for 15 minutes, then turn out to cool completely. Ice cake and refrigerate for 1 hour before serving.

"Montana" is the state song for the State of Montana. Two gifted individuals, noted songwriter, Joseph E. Howard and Butte newspaper city editor, Charles C. Cohan, composed "Montana" some 80 years ago in Butte. They dedicated the song to the Montana Children's Home and Hospital, now known as Shodair Hospital in Helena.

FUDGE CAKE

"always a favorite"

1 cup butter
2 cups sugar
4 squares melted chocolate
4 egg yolks
2 cups flour
1 cup milk
2 teaspoons vanilla
1/2 cup nuts
4 beaten egg whites

Cream sugar and butter, add egg yolks and melted chocolate. Add rest of ingredients, adding beaten egg whites last. Bake at 350 degrees in a 9x13 inch greased and floured pan for 45 minutes or until toothpick comes out clean. Frost with your favorite chocolate frosting.

SWEET TREATS

Manufacturing got its start in 1845 when Father Anthony Ravalli arrived from Europe bringing two grinding stones with him to St. Mary's mission. The first flour mills were established. Flour soon became a surplus and was sold to the American Fur Company posts along the Missouri River.

ROSE ROSS'S ICE WATER CAKE

"served to the officers at Fort Mammoth, YSNP"

1/2 cup butter
1 1/2 cups sugar
2 1/2 cups cake flour before sifted
1 cup ice water or very cold water
2 teaspoons baking powder
5 egg whites
1/2 teaspoon salt
2 teaspoons vanilla
1/4 teaspoon almond extract

Cream butter and sugar well. Add water and flour alternately. Always add water first, then flour. Mix each addition until blended. Add egg whites, stiffly beaten, last. Fold in gently until blended. Grease and flour two 9-inch cake pans or one 9x13 inch pan. Bake at 375 degrees 25-30 minutes. Frost with a boiled frosting or a seven-minute frosting. The leftover egg yolks can be used in a sponge cake or noodles.

On July 2, 1860, the Steamship Chippewa reached Fort Benton and proved that the channel of the Missouri was navigable to that point - just in time to serve all the gold camps springing up in southwestern Montana.

MEXICAN NUT CAKE

10 eggs, separated
1 1/4 cups sugar
1 cup nuts, chopped
1 teaspoon vanilla
1 teaspoon cream of tartar
6 tablespoons flour

Beat yolks and sugar for 20 minutes. Add cream of tartar, vanilla, and flour to the chopped nuts. Beat egg whites until stiff. Add yolk and sugar mixture to the nut mixture. Fold in egg whites. Pour into round angel food cake pan. Bake at 350 degrees for 50-60 minutes. Turn upside down and allow to cool completely before removing from pan.

Hundreds of spectators attend the Miles City Bucking Horse Sale held annually in May. They say the one that bucks the hardest sells for the most money. Up to World War I, horse raising was a major industry in Montana and by 1918, Miles City was the largest market in the world.

APPLE CAKE AND RUM SAUCE

1/4 cup butter
1 cup sugar
1 egg
1 2/3 cups chopped juicy apples
1 cup flour
1 teaspoon cinnamon
1/2 teaspoon nutmeg
1 teaspoon baking soda (scant)
1/2 teaspoon salt
1 teaspoon vanilla

Sauce:
1/2 cup brown sugar
1/4 cup white sugar
1/4 cup butter
1/2 cup milk or half and half
1 teaspoon rum flavoring

Cream butter and sugar, add egg. Sift dry ingredients. Add to creamed mixture. Fold in chopped apples. Bake in 8x8 inch prepared pan at 350 degrees for 45 minutes. Bring sauce mixture just to a boil and remove from heat. Serve over cake, either warm or cool.

SWEET TREATS

Glacier National Park lives up to its name with its fifty living glaciers. It lies in the Northern most section of the Rocky Mountains and is "naturally inviting" to anyone that enjoys scenery, backpacking, or a picnic lunch (no bears invited, please).

POPPY SEED CAKE

1 package cake mix
(yellow, white, or lemon)
1/2 cup oil
1 package lemon instant pudding
(3 ounce size)
4 eggs
1 cup water
3 or 4 tablespoons poppy seeds

Mix together and pour into greased bundt pan. Bake at 350 degrees for 45-55 minutes, using the toothpick test.

Look north from just about any spot in Helena and you will see a landform that looks like a big friendly fellow lying on his back catching a wink or two. He has been nicknamed "Sleeping Giant". His feet point toward the Continental Divide and his head toward the Gates of the Mountains. He hasn't always looked like this, it just happened after his "second nose" fell off when a possible earthquake may have occurred on February 4, 1878.

COCONUT POUND CAKE

1 1/3 cups vegetable oil
2 1/4 cups sugar
5 eggs
3 cups flour
1 teaspoon baking powder
1/4 teaspoon salt
2 teaspoons coconut extract
1 cup milk
1 cup shredded coconut

Cream oil and sugar together. Add eggs, one at a time. Mix after each, then beat on high speed for 10 minutes. Sift dry ingredients together and add to creamed mixture. Add extract and milk. Fold in coconut. Pour into greased bundt pan. Bake at 325 degrees for 1 hour and 15 minutes or until toothpick comes out clean. Begin check after 1 hour.

With Montana's diversified climate and regions, there are more than 2,000 species of wildflowers and non-flowering plants growing on the mountainsides, valleys, and prairies. The poppy, primrose, daisy, and aster are some that are used for the beautiful bouquets that grace Montana homes.

WHITE CAKE-LOVER'S DREAM

1 1/2 cups sugar
1/2 cup butter (scant, creamed well)
1 cup cold water (scant)
1 teaspoon vanilla
2 cups cake flour (measure before sifting)
2 teaspoons baking powder
1/2 teaspoon salt
5 egg whites, beaten stiff

Cream butter well. Add sugar gradually. Sift flour, baking powder, and salt and add to creamed butter and sugar mixture alternately with water. Add flavoring. Fold in beaten egg whites. Pour into two 8-inch prepared cake pans. Bake for 30-35 minutes at 350 degrees. This cake can be filled between layers with lemon filling, frosted with 7-minute frosting and sprinkled with coconut.

Senior Citizen Centers are springing up in many Montana towns where cards, dances, crafts, and other organized entertainment is inviting to seniors of Montana. Many of these folks could teach the young'uns how to do a polka, schottische, and an old time waltz.

PARTY CAKE

"a keeper"

1 box of yellow cake mix (with pudding and butter flavor).
Bake according to directions, using a prepared 9x13 inch cake pan.

Five minutes before cake is done, prepare the following:

1 16-ounce can crushed pineapple with juice
1 cup white sugar

Bring to a full boil and boil 30 seconds.

When cake is done, remove from oven and while cake is still hot, poke holes (a lot) in cake with a fork or handle of wooden spoon. Immediately pour pineapple mixture (hot) over cake.

LET CAKE COOL COMPLETELY at room temperature.

Mix **1 large package INSTANT vanilla pudding** according to directions and spread over cake. Refrigerate until pudding is set.

Spread **1 8-ounce carton whipped topping** on cake and sprinkle top with **shredded coconut** and **chopped nuts** (optional). This can be done right before serving. If making the cake a day ahead of time, cover well in refrigerator so pudding will not get crusty.

Lewis and Clark named the three rivers that branch out at Three Forks for the three men that were instrumental in promoting the Lewis and Clark Expedition: the Jefferson, for President Thomas Jefferson; the Madison, for Secretary of State, James Madison; and the Gallatin, for Secretary of the Treasury, Albert Gallatin.

NO-FAIL DEVILS FOOD

"an all time family favorite"

2 cups sugar
1/2 cup shortening or margarine
2 eggs
1/2 cup sour milk
2 teaspoons vanilla
1 1/2 teaspoons baking soda
2 heaping cups flour
2 squares chocolate
1 cup boiling water

Add all ingredients in the order given; melting chocolate squares in the boiling water. Pour into 9x13 inch prepared pan and bake for 30 minutes at 350 degrees using the toothpick test. Frost with your favorite frosting.

On July 28, 1862, Montana hit its first major gold strike on Grasshopper Creek. John White's discovery brought Bannack, a mining camp, into existence and the gold rush was on; bringing in hundreds of miners within a short time. Bannack later became Montana's first territorial capital.

RHUBARB CAKE

5 cups chopped rhubarb
1 3-ounce strawberry or raspberry gelatin
1 cup sugar
3 cups miniature marshmallows
1 cup broken nutmeats
1 package white or yellow cake mix

Place rhubarb in bottom of greased 9x13 inch cake pan. Sprinkle gelatin over rhubarb. Top with sugar, then sprinkle marshmallows and nuts. Prepare cake mix according to package directions, pour over all. Bake for 1 hour at 350 degrees. Let cool a few minutes, invert on foil and serve with whipped cream or ice cream.

CHRISTMAS RUM CAKE

1 box yellow cake mix
1 box (3 ounce size) vanilla instant pudding mix
1/2 cup light rum
1/2 cup water
1/2 cup vegetable oil
4 eggs
1 cup chopped pecans

Rum Glaze:
1/2 cup butter
1 cup white sugar
1/2 cup water
1/4 cup rum

Combine cake mix, pudding mix, rum, water, vegetable oil, and eggs. Beat for 2 minutes. Add 1/2 cup pecans to the batter. Put remaining 1/2 cup pecans in the bottom of a greased and floured bundt pan. Pour batter over nuts. Bake at 325 degrees in preheated oven for 50-70 minutes, using the toothpick test. When cake is done, remove from pan and allow to cool for 30 minutes. Pour hot rum glaze over cake. Be sure to use all of the glaze. Put on serving platter, cake will settle.

Glaze: Melt butter in saucepan. Add sugar and water, stir and bring to a boil. Cook until slightly syrupy. Remove from heat. When cake is ready for glazing, add rum. Pour immediately over partially cooled cake.

SWEET TREATS

Summer in Montana is a time for all kinds of festivities. Usually with most events, a parade is on the agenda. Clowns, cowboys riding their favorite horses, a band playing a lively Sousa march, and the "Red, White, and Blue" coming down the street - an exciting and proud time for the young and the old alike.

STRAWBERRY CAKE

"a fun summer dessert"

1 white cake mix (regular size)
1 3-ounce box strawberry gelatin
1 cup salad oil
3/4 cup water
4 eggs
1 16-ounce bag thawed frozen strawberries
(save 1/4 of the strawberries for frosting)

Mix well, pour into 9x13 inch greased and floured cake pan. Bake at 350 degrees for 40 minutes or until toothpick comes out clean.

Frosting:
1 8-ounce package cream cheese
1/2 cup margarine, softened
2 teaspoons vanilla
4 cups powdered sugar (sifted)
1/4 package strawberries (from above)

Mix well, spread on cake. Garnish with fresh strawberry halves and keep in cool place until ready to serve.

CRAZY CAKE
"worth the work"

3 cups unsifted flour
2 teaspoons baking soda
2 cups sugar
1 teaspoon salt
1/3 cup cocoa

Mix dry ingredients together in 9x13 inch pan.

1 cup salad oil (scant)
2 cups cold water
2 tablespoons vinegar
1 teaspoon vanilla

Mix wet ingredients together. Pour over dry mixture. Stir just until well blended. Bake at 350 degrees for 35-40 minutes. While cake is baking, make filling.

Filling:
1 cup milk
3/4 cup butter
4 tablespoons flour (heaping)
1 1/2 cups sugar
1/8 teaspoon salt
2 teaspoons vanilla

Blend dry ingredients thoroughly; then add butter, milk, and vanilla. Cook until thick. When cake is partially cool, spread filling on top.

Topping:
1 cup sugar
1/4 cup milk
1/4 cup butter
1 tablespoon corn syrup
2 tablespoons cocoa

Boil to soft stage then remove from stove and beat until thick. Drizzle over top of cake and filling.

SWEET TREATS

Hearing the ducks and geese as they head south for the winter always brings a glimpse towards the sky in the fall. More of a welcoming sound and sight is the returning of the migrating birds to Montana in the spring of the year. These birds fly with endurance, forming a "V Shape" to better their time. It is customary to switch leaders and you will notice that one side of the "V" is seldom complete.

SALLY'S ORANGE CHIFFON CAKE

2 1/4 cups sifted cake flour
1 1/2 cups sugar
3 teaspoons baking powder
1 teaspoon salt
1/2 cup cooking oil
5 egg yolks, unbeaten
3/4 cup orange juice
1 cup egg whites (7 or 8 eggs)
1/2 teaspoon cream of tartar

Sift together in bowl: cake flour, sugar, baking powder, and salt. Make "well" and add in order: cooking oil, unbeaten egg yolks, and orange juice. Beat until smooth. Measure into large mixing bowl, egg whites and cream of tartar. Beat until whites form very stiff peaks. Pour egg yolk mixture gradually over beaten whites, gently folding with rubber scraper just until blended. Pour into ungreased tube pan. Bake at 325 degrees for 55 minutes, then at 350 degrees for 10-15 minutes or until top springs back when lightly touched. Invert on funnel. Let hang until cool.

SPICE CAKE

1 1/2 cups brown sugar
1/2 cup butter or margarine
2 eggs, beaten
1/2 cup sour cream
2 cups flour
1 teaspoon baking soda
1 teaspoon baking powder
2 teaspoons cinnamon
1 teaspoon cloves
1/2 teaspoon nutmeg
1/2 teaspoon salt
1 cup raisins (optional)
1 cup chopped nuts

Cream sugar and butter together. Add beaten eggs. Sift dry ingredients together and alternate with sour cream when adding to creamed mixture. Add nuts and raisins. Bake in prepared 9x13 inch pan at 350 degrees for about 40 minutes or until toothpick inserted in center of cake comes out clean.

EASY PENUCHE ICING

1/2 cup butter
1/4 cup milk
1/2 teaspoon salt
1 cup brown sugar (packed)
1 3/4 to 2 cups sifted, powdered sugar

Melt butter in saucepan. Add brown sugar. Boil over low heat 2 minutes, stirring constantly. Stir in milk. Bring to boil, stirring constantly. Cool to lukewarm. Gradually add sugar. Beat until thick enough to spread. If icing becomes stiff, add a little hot water.

SWEET TREATS

County fairs, during the summer months in Montana, are a fun place to be; a place where you see many of your old friends and meet new ones. Much visiting goes on between eating a good Montana beef hamburger and a ride on the ferris wheel.

OATMEAL CAKE

Mix the following together:
1 cube butter
1 cup long cooking oatmeal
1 1/2 cups boiling water

Let stand 20 minutes then add and mix:

2 eggs
1 cup white sugar
1 cup brown sugar
1 1/3 cups flour
1/2 teaspoon salt
1 teaspoon baking soda
1 teaspoon cinnamon

Grease and flour 9x13 inch cake pan. Bake at 350 degrees for 30-35 minutes. Remove cooked cake from oven and spread topping over top while cake is still hot. Place under broiler for 3-4 minutes, watching closely to avoid scorching.

Topping: Mix together:
4 to 6 tablespoons butter
1/2 cup sugar (brown or white)
1/4 to 1/2 cup condensed milk
1 cup shredded coconut
1 cup chopped nuts

"Big Sky Country" has become a slogan for the state of Montana, referring to the immense area of mountains, valleys, and blue sky. People love the Big Sky way of life.

CHOCOLATE SHEET CAKE

"excellent for a pot luck"

2 cups flour
2 cups sugar
1/2 cup shortening
1 cube margarine
1 cup water
4 tablespoons cocoa
1/2 cup buttermilk
2 eggs
1 teaspoon baking soda
1/2 teaspoon salt
1 teaspoon vanilla

Place margarine, shortening, and water in small saucepan. Bring to a full boil. Remove from stove. In a large bowl, mix cocoa, flour, and sugar. Pour the hot mixture over the dry ingredients and stir. Add remaining ingredients, mixing well. Pour into a greased 10x15 inch cake pan or jelly roll pan. Bake at 375 degrees for 20 minutes, or until toothpick inserted in center comes out clean. Ten minutes before cake is done, make frosting.

Frosting:
1/2 cup margarine
4 tablespoons cocoa
5 tablespoons milk
1 teaspoon vanilla
3 to 3 1/2 cups powdered sugar
1 cup chopped walnuts or pecans

Bring milk, cocoa, and margarine to a boil in a small saucepan. Remove from heat and add vanilla, powdered sugar, and nuts. Beat together and spread over warm cake.

SWEET TREATS

In June of 1864, Sidney Edgerton was appointed by President Abraham Lincoln to be Montana's first territorial governor. After a stormy two years in office, he was forced to resign in early 1866.

CHRISTMAS FRUITCAKE

Add the following together in large bowl, whole, do not chop or dice.
1 pound dates (seeded)
1 pound green cherries
1 pound red cherries
1 pound pineapple, yellow (glazed)
3/4 pound walnuts (3 cups)
3/4 pound Brazil nuts (3 cups)

Mix together and add to above mixture:
1/2 cup sugar
4 eggs, beaten
1 1/2 cups flour

There is just enough batter to hold the fruit together so it must be mixed very well. Grease 4 small loaf pans (8x4" by 2 1/2") and bake at 325 degrees for about 1 hour and 20 minutes, depending on the size of your pans. Check with toothpick for doneness. (The size of the pan is optional.)

Big Sky Resort, located south of Bozeman, was Chet Huntley's dream. Born in Cardwell, Montana, the late television newscaster loved the area and began development of the surroundings with the plan being announced to the public February 16, 1970. A recreation area has been created to include winter and summer activities.

RICH CHOCOLATE CUPCAKES

1 1/4 cups unsifted flour
1 cup sugar
1/3 cup cocoa
3/4 teaspoon baking soda
1/2 teaspoon salt
1 cup buttermilk
1/3 cup vegetable oil
1 egg
1 teaspoon vanilla

Combine flour, sugar, cocoa, baking soda, and salt. Add buttermilk, oil, egg, and vanilla. Blend well.

Filling:
1 8-ounce package cream cheese
1/3 cup sugar
1/8 teaspoon salt
1 egg
1/2 cup mini chocolate chips

Blend cream cheese, sugar, and salt. Add egg and beat until smooth. Stir in chips. Fill paper baking cups 1/2 full of first mixture, then add 1 tablespoon cheese filling. Bake at 350 degrees for 30 minutes or until tops are golden brown. Good with or without frosting.

The Rev. Pierre-Jean DeSmet was the first Jesuit missionary to arrive in Montana in 1840. He said his first mass near Three Forks and baptized over three hundred Indians. DeSmet was the founder of St. Mary's Mission in the Bitterroot Valley in 1841. Several other Jesuits came to Montana to work with the Indians and the whites; thus contributing to the religious development of the state.

ORANGE CHIFFON PIE

"truly a lovely dessert"

1 9-inch baked pie shell
1 cup white sugar
5 tablespoons flour
1 tablespoon cornstarch
1/4 teaspoon salt
1 tablespoon grated orange rind
2 cups orange juice
2 egg yolks
2 egg whites
1 tablespoon butter
2 teaspoons lemon juice

Mix sugar, flour, cornstarch, salt, and rind. Add juice and mix well. Cook over low heat until mixture thickens. Add beaten egg yolks, butter, and lemon juice. Remove from heat and fold in beaten egg whites. Pour into pie shell. Cool and serve with whipped cream.

Montana has several varieties of wild berries that are native to the state, such as huckleberry, buffalo berry, gooseberry, and the loganberry; just to name a few.

MONTANA BERRY PIE
"any Montana berry will do"

Crust:
2 cups flour
1 1/4 teaspoons salt
2 teaspoons sugar
2/3 cup salad oil
3 tablespoons milk

Mix flour, salt, sugar, oil, and milk together. Pat into 8x8 inch pan, reserving 1 cup of the mixture to sprinkle on top. This crust does not require a rolling pin.

Filling:
4 cups berries
1 cup sugar
1/4 cup flour
1/4 teaspoon cinnamon
1/8 teaspoon nutmeg
1/8 teaspoon cloves
2 tablespoons butter or margarine

Mix berries and dry ingredients. Pour over crust and dot with butter. Sprinkle reserved mixture on top. Bake at 400 degrees for 40 to 50 minutes.

The Lewis and Clark Caverns State Park, located near Three Forks, is one of nature's underground mysteries. Many stalagmites, stalactites, and columns form interesting formations. The cave is still very much in its natural state.

ZUCCHINI PIE

5 cups zucchini, peeled, seeded, sliced
1 1/4 cups sugar
1 1/2 tablespoons flour
1 1/2 teaspoons cream of tartar
1 teaspoon cinnamon
Dash of salt
1 tablespoon lemon juice
1 tablespoon vanilla
1 can crushed pineapple (8 1/2 ounce, drained)
1 egg, beaten

Cook zucchini in water to cover. Simmer until fork tender. Drain and cool. Add remaining ingredients and bake in unbaked "Never Fail" pie crust for 40 minutes at 350 degrees. Remove from oven. Sprinkle Streusel Topping on top. Bake at 350 degrees for about 20 more minutes.

STREUSEL TOPPING

1 1/2 cups bread crumbs
1/2 cup brown sugar
1/4 cup soft margarine
Dash of cinnamon

Combine until crumbly. Follow above directions.

Summer in Montana: "Montana summers are as famous for their unabashed frenzy as they are for their short duration. Summer is, after all, the most exciting day of the year." (Dean Krakel II, Outside, Oct./Nov., 1979).

MONTANA STRAWBERRY PIE

1 baked 9-inch pie shell
1 quart fresh strawberries
1 cup sugar
3 tablespoons cornstarch
2 tablespoons lemon juice

Crush half of strawberries; stir in cornstarch, sugar, and lemon juice. Cook over moderate heat until clear and thickened. Cool. Cut rest of strawberries in halves and place in baked pie shell (save a few for garnish). Pour mixture over berries and top the pie with whipped cream.

Montana sapphires are the official gemstones for the State of Montana and have been mined in several areas throughout the state. Yogo Mine, located near Lewistown, is world famous for its sapphires. Gemologists consider them to be the standard by which sapphires, the world over, are judged.

CHOCOLATE ICE CREAM CHEESE PIE

Crust: Makes 2
1 package chocolate cake mix
3/4 cup ready to spread fudge frosting
3/4 cup water
1/4 cup oil

Generously grease bottom, sides and rim of two 9-inch pie pans. In large bowl, blend cake mix, frosting, water, and salad oil. Beat 2 minutes at high speed. Spread 1/2 batter in bottom of each pan. Do not spread up sides of pans. Bake at 350 degrees for 25-30 minutes. Do not overbake. Cakes will collapse to form shells. Cool completely.

Filling:
1 quart softened chocolate ice cream
1 8-ounce package softened cream cheese
3 1-ounce squares sweet chocolate, grated
1/2 cup slivered almonds, toasted

Beat cream cheese until fluffy. Blend in ice cream. Fold in grated chocolate and almonds. Spoon into crusts and freeze. Stand at room temperature 30 to 40 minutes before slicing. Serve with a bit of whipped cream on top.

Lucia Darling opened one of Montana's first schools in Bannack in 1863. Parents had to pay directly for their children's schooling. In Nevada City, Kate Dunlap operated another school much the same. Virginia City was the first community to set up a public school district in 1866.

MOM'S APPLE PIE

"it looks good enough for McCall's"

Pastry for two crust pie
5 cups apples
(pared and sliced)
2 1/2 tablespoons flour
1 cup sugar
1 teaspoon cinnamon
1/4 teaspoon nutmeg
2 tablespoons butter

Line a 9-inch pie pan with pastry dough. Mix flour, sugar, and spices, adding apples to mixture. Fill pan with apple mixture. Place butter in dots on top. Moisten edge of lower crust. Cover with top crust which has been perforated. Flute edge and trim off excess dough. Bake for 50 minutes at 400 degrees.

Glendive has become a "Caviar Capital". An average of 1,700 female paddlefish are caught each year on the Yellowstone River and the eggs are shipped to various buyers throughout the United States and Europe with the "Made in Montana, U.S.A." stamp enclosed.

SOUR CREAM RAISIN PIE

1 9-inch baked pie shell
2 cups raisins
2 cups water
1 cup brown sugar
2 heaping tablespoons flour
1 cup sour cream
1/4 teaspoon cinnamon
3 egg yolks
1/4 cube butter
Pinch of salt

Boil raisins for 15 minutes in the 2 cups of water. Let stand until ready to use. Mix in order: sugar, flour, sour cream, cinnamon, egg yolks, cooked raisins, and their juice, butter, and salt. Cook until thick. Put in a baked pie shell. Bake at 350 degrees for 8-10 minutes. Remove from oven and top with meringue and bake as directed.

Meringue: Beat **3 egg whites** and add **6 tablespoons sugar** gradually, beating until stiff. Spread over pie filling and bake at 350 degrees until lightly brown, about 10-12 minutes.

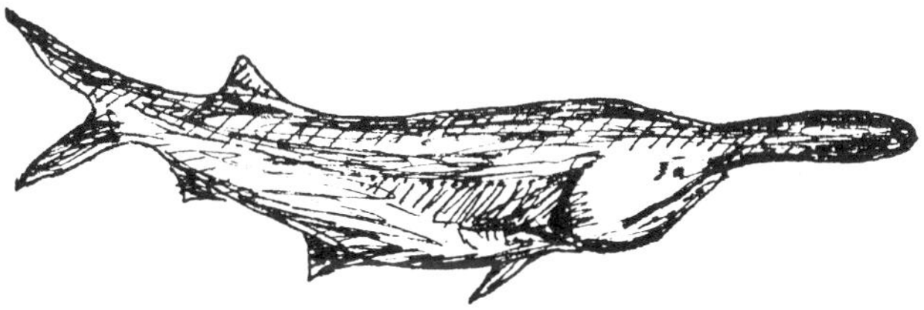

Small town Montana cafes are usually a gathering place for many of the local farmers and ranchers. Many problems and solutions are hashed over while consuming several cups of coffee. It's a good way to say "howdy" to your friends and it makes the work day seem just a bit shorter.

COCONUT CREAM PIE

1 baked 9-inch pie shell
3/4 cup sugar
1/3 cup flour or 3 tablespoons cornstarch
1/2 teaspoon salt
2 cups milk
3 slightly beaten egg yolks
2 tablespoons butter
1 teaspoon vanilla
1 cup flaked coconut

Combine sugar, flour, and salt. Gradually stir in milk. Cook and stir over medium heat until bubbly. Cook and stir 2 minutes. Remove from heat. Stir small amount of hot mix into egg yolks, immediately return to hot mixture. Cook 2 minutes, stirring constantly. Remove from heat. Add butter, vanilla, and coconut. Pour into baked pie shell. Top with meringue or whipped cream.

Jeannette Rankin, a young University of Montana graduate, became the first woman ever elected to the U.S. Congress. She was elected November 6, 1916. She fought hard for women's rights. She also was one of the nation's leading pacifists, voting against America's entry into two world wars. "She opened the door of political opportunity for all American women," is a quote from Thomas "Tip" O'Neill, Jr. during a tribute paid to her in 1985. Jeannette Rankin died in 1973 at the age of 92.

APPLE PUDDING

4 eggs, beat until creamy
1 1/2 cups sugar
2/3 cup flour
1 teaspoon baking powder

Mix sugar with eggs until well mixed. Add flour and baking powder

Fold the following into above mixture:
2 cups chopped apple
1 cup chopped walnuts
1 teaspoon vanilla
Add a suspicion of nutmeg, if desired

Bake at 325 degrees for 40 minutes in 9x13 inch buttered pan. A dollop of whipped cream or ice cream is nice for an added touch.

The passenger train, Amtrak, runs along the Hi-Line in northern Montana. The stations are located in small towns, portraying a Norman Rockwell painting. Traveling through Montana, heading west, the traveler will experience a scenic mountainous route and traveling east you will be able to enjoy the wide open spaces of the Big Sky.

RABARBERGROD - RHUBARB PUDDING

1 1/2 pounds rhubarb
1 1/4 quarts water,
less if using frozen rhubarb
2 cups sugar
2 teaspoons red food coloring
or 1/2 cup cinnamon candies
6 teaspoons cornstarch or
potato flour

Cut up rhubarb and cook until tender. Put through a sieve. This will make 4 cups strained rhubarb. Add sugar, coloring or candies. Heat. Mix cornstarch or flour with a little cold water and add. Cook until thick and smooth. Serve cold with thin cream. This keeps well in covered container in refrigerator.

SWEET TREATS

With Montana's early history of gold mines, gold strikes, and gold seekers; there are several ghost towns where gold rushes had come into existence. A trek through these towns will dig up stories of what it was like in those days of vicious crimes, early deaths, dance hall girls, saloons, and long hard work. Not all of the towns are ghost towns as a few of them still have residents living there and some of the buildings have been restored.

BREAD PUDDING

2 cups milk
1/4 cup butter
3 cups soft bread crumbs
(3 to 4 slices of bread)
1/2 cup sugar
1 teaspoon cinnamon
1/4 teaspoon salt
2 eggs, slightly beaten
1/2 cup raisins

Heat milk and butter over medium heat until butter is melted and milk is scalded. Mix remaining ingredients in ungreased 1 1/2 quart casserole and stir in milk mixture. Place casserole in pan of very hot water (1 inch deep). Bake at 350 degrees for about 40 minutes or until knife inserted one inch from edge of pudding comes out clean.

The Homestead Era began when Congress initiated the 1862 Homestead Act which enabled settlers to claim 160 acres of government land as his own. If he lived on it and worked it, the land became his, practically free, after a five year period. David Carpenter became the first person in Montana to take advantage of the 1862 Act when he filed claim for land near Helena on August 1, 1868.

ROMMEGROT

"Norwegian brides serve this
to their grooms on their wedding day"

In large saucepan, blend together **2 cups dairy sour cream** and **1/2 cup water**. Place over medium-low heat, cook and stir until sour cream separates, about 15 minutes. Mix **1/2 cup flour** and **1/2 teaspoon salt**. Blend in **1 cup cold water** to flour and salt mixture. Stir into the sour cream. Cook and stir over medium heat until thickened and bubbly. Gradually blend in **2 cups warmed milk**. Pour into bowl. Dot with **2 tablespoons butter**. Sprinkle with mixture of **1/4 cup sugar** and **1/4 teaspoon cinnamon**. Serve warm.

Chinook winds blow across Montana in January and February. These warm winds have saved many cattle as they melt the snow and make it possible for the livestock to reach the grass. The Indian word chinook means "snow eater." It was Charles M. Russell's postcard picture of a starving range cow, "Waiting for a Chinook", that first won him recognition as an artist.

FANNIE FARMER FUDGE

"could this be the secret recipe?"

Combine:
2 cups white sugar
1 6-ounce can evaporated milk
10 marshmallows

Cook for 7 minutes from the time it comes to full rolling boil. Stir on low heat to avoid scorching.

Add:
1 6-ounce package chocolate chips
1/4 pound of butter
1 cup chopped nuts
1 teaspoon vanilla

Mix well. Pour into buttered 8x8 inch pan and set in refrigerator for 24 hours.

Soldier's Chapel, located at Big Sky, was built as a war memorial for the 163rd Infantry of World War II. The chapel has elegant stained glass windows and a beautiful view of Lone Mountain. Many couples choose the chapel as a setting for their wedding day.

MILLION DOLLAR FUDGE

1 2/3 cups (13-ounce can) evaporated milk
1 2/3 cups (7-ounce jar) marshmallow cream
4 cups granulated sugar
1 tablespoon butter or margarine
2 cups (12-ounce package) semi-sweet chocolate chips
2 Hershey bars, broken in pieces
1 teaspoon vanilla
1 2/3 cups chopped pecans

Combine evaporated milk, marshmallow cream, sugar, and butter in a heavy 4-quart saucepan. Cook over medium heat, stirring constantly until mixture comes to a full rolling boil; boil and stir 7 minutes. Remove from heat; immediately add chocolate chips and Hershey bars, beating until completely melted. Blend in the vanilla and nuts. Pour the mixture into 9x9 inch buttered pan. Cut into squares when cool.

SWEET TREATS

The Continental Divide winds through Montana separating the waters running west into the Pacific Ocean from those that run east to the Atlantic. Most of Montana lies east of the divide.

BOSTON CREAM LOAF

4 cups sugar
2 cups cream
2/3 cup light corn syrup
1/4 teaspoon salt

Slowly boil above ingredients to a softball stage. Let stand until mixture cools to lukewarm, then add:

1 package candied cherries (red or green)
1 package candied pineapple (red or green)
2 cups chopped walnuts
1/4 cup butter
2 teaspoons vanilla

Stir until mixture looses its gloss, then pour into 9x13 inch buttered pan, refrigerate and cut into 1-inch squares when cooled. These may also be dipped into melted chocolate for delicious homemade chocolates.

DIVINITY

5 cups white sugar
1 cup light corn syrup
1 cup water
2 egg whites (room temperature)
2 cups coarsely chopped nuts
1/2 cup dried candied cherries (optional)
1/2 teaspoon vanilla extract

Combine sugar, corn syrup, and water in heavy 3-quart saucepan. Bring to boil, stirring constantly. Continue boiling to 236-238 degrees until a small amount of the mixture forms a soft ball in cold water. Place egg whites in large bowl and beat until foamy. Add salt and beat until stiff enough to stand in peaks. Slowly pour syrup into egg whites while continuing to beat until mixture holds its shape. Fold nuts, cherries, and vanilla into egg white mixture. Drop in mounds quickly from a teaspoon onto greased baking sheet or wax paper. Let stand until pieces are no longer sticky and are of uniform consistency throughout.

SWEET TREATS

On July 25, 1806, the Lewis and Clark Exhibition was traveling down the Yellowstone River. William Clark noticed a huge unusual rock formation located in the river that towered up about 200 feet. Clark etched his name and date and named the rock "Pompey's Pillar" after Sacajawea's son, "Little Pomp." The historic landmark was purchased by the Bureau of Land Management and recently opened to the public. The signature is the only remaining physical evidence of the Lewis and Clark Expedition of 1804-1806. The site is located about 28 miles east of Billings.

PEANUT BRITTLE

2 cups sugar
1 cup white corn syrup
2 cups raw peanuts
1/2 cup water
1/2 teaspoon salt
2 tablespoons butter
2 teaspoons vanilla
2 teaspoons baking soda

Cook sugar, syrup, salt, and water together to form a hard ball when dropped in cold water (about 260 degrees). Add butter and peanuts, cook until syrup is a golden brown (300 degrees). Remove from stove and add vanilla and soda. Stir and pour on buttered cookie sheet immediately. When cool, break into pieces. (An iron skillet or heavy saucepan is suggested to cook this in.)

CRAZY CORN

2 quarts popped corn
1 1/3 cups nuts
1 1/3 cups sugar
1 cup butter
1/2 cup light corn syrup
1 teaspoon vanilla

Combine popped corn and nuts in a large roasting pan. Cook sugar, butter, and syrup in a heavy saucepan; stirring all of the time. Cook just past soft ball stage (240 degrees). Add vanilla and pour over popcorn mixture, stirring to coat well. Turn out on wax paper to cool.

POPCORN BALLS

5 quarts popped corn
2 cups sugar
1 1/2 cups water
1/2 teaspoon salt
1/2 cup light corn syrup
1 teaspoon vinegar
1 teaspoon vanilla

Pop corn and keep warm in 300 degree oven. Cook all ingredients except vinegar and vanilla in sauce pan until it reaches hard ball stage. Add vinegar and vanilla and cook a short time longer. Slowly pour over popped corn, stirring in syrup. Using butter on hands, quickly press into balls. Wrap with saran wrap.

SWEET TREATS

"Cabin Fever" sometimes sets in for Montana folk, especially in winter when the snow stacks high and travel seems to be out of the question. Entertaining the family sometimes consists of playing a game of cards or board games and cooking up a batch of taffy.

STUB'S TAFFY
"a family favorite"

2 cups white sugar
1 cup white syrup
1/4 teaspoon baking soda
1 tablespoon butter
1 tablespoon vinegar

Mix ingredients in heavy saucepan; stir over low heat until sugar is dissolved. Boil over medium heat until a small bit put in a cup of cold water is brittle and will break with a snap, about 265 degrees on a candy thermometer. Pour on a buttered platter and pull when cool enough to handle. Pull until taffy turns almost white in color, then stretch into a rope about 1-inch thick and twist. Cut into small pieces. Wrap individually in wax paper.

PERSONAL FAVORITES

Notes & Recipes:

ROUNDUP

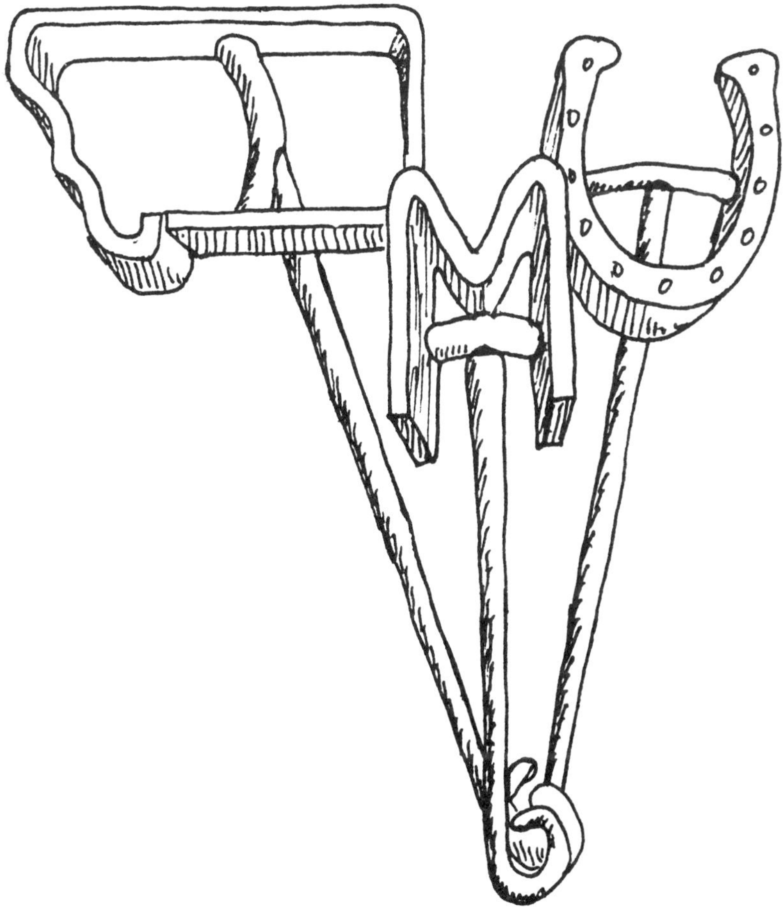

ROUNDUP

On July 14, 1864, "Four Georgians", as they were called, decided to take one last chance at prospecting near Prickly Pear Valley. They hit upon a prosperous strike and named it "Last Chance Gulch", which later became Helena. The thoroughfare, Last Chance Gulch, exists in Helena, where you can view many old buildings dating back to the 1870's.

CANNED PIE APPLES

2 1/2 gallons of peeled, sliced apples
5 cups sugar

Layer in large crock or plastic container by using 1 quart of apples with 1/2 cup sugar sprinkled on top until 10 quarts of apples are used. Press down, cover and let stand overnight. Pack in 1-quart jars, seal and process in boiling water bath for 15 minutes.

This is a wonderful way to use apples when there has been a good crop. For apple pie, use one quart and proceed as you would for a fresh apple pie - also excellent for cobblers. There will be excess juice - this can be made into apple syrup. Yield: 7 quarts.

ROUNDUP

The State Fair is held in Great Falls in late July. The exhibits bring people in from throughout the state where talented and productive Montanans display their entries with anticipation of a blue ribbon. The State Fair Race Meet sponsors horse racing in June and July along with five days of racing during the fair. The $100,000 Budweiser Derby for 3-year olds is scheduled and is the richest race in Montana for older horses.

CUCUMBER SLICES

"the best and easiest ever"

6 cups thinly sliced cucumbers
1 cup thinly sliced onions
2 cups sugar
1 cup vinegar
1 1/2 teaspoons salt
1 teaspoon celery salt
1 teaspoon mustard seed

Wash cucumbers, do not peel. Slice. Mix the vinegar and sugar and pour over the cucumbers and onions. Add the rest of the ingredients to the cucumber mixture. Stir occasionally for about 1 hour to dissolve the sugar. Cover tightly and refrigerate. These pickles keep well and are crisp. (A discarded pickle jar with lid makes a nice container.)

ROUNDUP

The annual Montana Seed Show, held in Harlem in early March, is the only event of this sort left in Montana. Features are the seed exhibits plus quilts, cars, wool, and the traditional bake-offs. An art auction is also a popular part of the Seed Show.

NEVER-FAIL PIE CRUST

"a recipe for a new bride"

Yield: 3 pie shells

1 1/4 cups shortening
3 cups flour
1 teaspoon salt
1 egg at room temperature
5 tablespoons water
1 tablespoon vinegar

Cut shortening into flour and salt with a pastry blender until the size of peas. In another bowl; mix egg, water and vinegar together. Add to flour mixture just until well mixed. Divide into three equal parts and refrigerate for a few minutes. Roll into three 9-inch shells; fit into pie plates and perforate. Bake at 375 degrees for 15-20 minutes.

EGG WHITE TOPPING

"a special meringue"

1/2 cup water
Dash of salt
6 tablespoons white sugar
1 tablespoon cornstarch
3 egg whites, beaten

Mix the first four ingredients in double boiler. Cook until thick and clear. Beat egg whites until frothy. Continue beating while slowly pouring cooked mixture over egg whites. Continue beating for 5 minutes. Cover a filled pie shell with this mixture. Bake at 450 degrees for 5 to 7 minutes till golden brown.

ROUNDUP

Mountain sheep, antelope, elk, white tailed deer, mule deer, black and brown bear, and moose tally up the list for big game in Montana. Big game hunting brought the first tourists to Montana as early as 1855. In 1905, Montana's first resident hunting and fishing licenses were sold for $1.00 per family.

BEAR SAUSAGE AND CHEESE BALLS

"tasty with scrambled eggs"

1 pound sausage, medium hot
1 pound sharp Cheddar cheese, grated
1 egg, beaten
1/4 cup milk
3 cups biscuit mix

Mix all together by hand and drop by teaspoon onto ungreased cookie sheet. Bake at 325 degrees for 20-25 minutes or until golden brown. These freeze well, before or after baking.

ROUNDUP

Montana is a hunter's paradise. Elk, deer, antelope, and bear are among the big game animals. Even buffalo are still hunted. When the "season" opens, space is usually saved in the freezer for some of the wild meat for the long winter. Montana cooks invent various ways to prepare it.

JERKY

Begin with a lean cut of meat. Remove all fat. Cut with grain into long narrow strips not more than 1/4 inch thick.

Seasoning for 1 pound of meat: combine **1 teaspoon salt, 1/4 teaspoon pepper, 1/2 teaspoon onion salt, 1/4 teaspoon garlic salt, 1/4 teaspoon Worcestershire sauce,** and **1 drop tabasco.** Stir together in medium bowl with a little water to dissolve.

Lay in the sliced meat - add enough water to cover. Weight down with small dish and refrigerate overnight. Drain and pat dry with paper towels. Lay strips on oven rack, close together but not overlapping. Set oven at 150 degrees (lowest temperature). Leave door slightly ajar for circulation. Place foil under to catch any drips. Bake 3 to 6 hours.

When meat is dark and dry and cracks sharply, but does not break; it is done. Cool. Pack in plastic bags or jars, airtight. This jerky may be frozen.

You may want to experiment by adding soy sauce or liquid smoke, oregano, thyme, basil, etc. Brush on and pound in with wooden mallet. A smoker in place of the oven method works nicely, using hickory chips. It gives the meat a special flavor.

ROUNDUP

Strip farming became an accepted method of growing wheat in northern Montana during the 1920's and 1930's. It is one method to arrest wind-caused soil erosion.

STIRRUM
"a German treat"

4 eggs
1/2 cup milk
2 teaspoons baking powder
Pinch of salt
1 1/2 cups flour

Mix to pancake dough consistency. Melt 1/2 cup shortening in pan. Add batter to fry. Keep turning and breaking until cooked through and is in small pieces. Serves 3-4. Suggestions for serving: Serve with German sausage and lettuce and cream salad. Also good dipped in white syrup.

ROUNDUP

Helena is the scene of the Montana Traditional Jazz Festival held every June. Bands from around the country set up at various downtown locations for a weekend of fine jazz music.

WATERMELON FRUIT BASKET

1 large watermelon, about 12 pounds
1 cantaloupe
1 cup pitted dark cherries
2 cups seedless grapes
1 pint fresh strawberries
2 cups drained chunk pineapple

Place melon with flattest side down. With a large knife, cut watermelon to make a basket, leaving middle portion in place to form handle. Scoop out melon balls with melon ball cutter, smoothing walls and underside of handle. Notch edges of basket. Scoop cantaloupe balls and rinse remaining fruits and let drip dry. Fill watermelon with fruit. Sprinkle with orange juice and powdered sugar shortly before serving. A variety of fruits may be used.

ROUNDUP

Biking through Montana has become a popular sport in the Big Sky with two National Parks to tour. The state's scenery is worth the trip for the two-wheeled traveler. A stop along one of the mountain streams is a nice break and a cool one if you care to get your feet wet.

CLAM SAUCE

1 cup finely chopped onion
2 cloves garlic, minced
6 tablespoons oil
1 1/3 cups chicken broth
2/3 cup white wine
6 tablespoons butter
1/2 teaspoon oregano leaves
1 12-ounce can minced clams (reserving 1/2 of the liquid)
2/3 cup grated Parmesan cheese

In medium skillet, cook onion and garlic over low heat in oil. Stir in chicken broth, wine, butter, oregano, dash of pepper, and reserved clam liquid. Cook over low heat, about 20 minutes. Add clams to sauce and cook just until thoroughly heated. Remove from heat; stir in Parmesan cheese. Serve over cooked pasta.

ROUNDUP

Tailgate parties are as popular at Montana colleges and universities as they are in the bigger cities. The Montana State Bobcats and the University of Montana Grizzlies have been rivals for years. The first Grizzly-Bobcat football game was played in the snow on November 26, 1897, with the Grizzlies winning 18-6.

STUFFED EGGS

6 hard cooked eggs, peeled, and cut in half
3 tablespoons mayonnaise
Dash of salt
1/4 teaspoon horseradish
3 tablespoons drained, chopped sweet pickles
1 teaspoon celery salt
Shake of pepper

Remove yolks, save egg whites. Mash yolks with mayonnaise. Add remaining ingredients. Mix well. Refill egg whites with egg yolk mixture. You may garnish tops with thin slices of pimento, black olive slices, or sprinkle with paprika. Makes 12 filled egg halves.

ROUNDUP

Chokecherries are plentiful in Montana and can be found on small trees in coulees and along creeks. After eating these small berries your throat becomes dry and a feeling of choking comes about. No need to worry, but you may need a drink of water. Thus, the so called name "chokecherry" came into existence.

CHOKECHERRY JELLY

4 1/2 cups chokecherry juice
4 cups sugar
1 lemon
1 package pectin

Combine chokecherry juice with cut up lemon in large kettle. Bring to boil. Boil 1 minute. Remove lemon, add pectin and bring to a full rolling boil for 1 minute. Pour into sterilized glasses and cover with paraffin.

thanks to all of these special cooks throughout Montana. Some are living on farms and hes, some are living in small towns, and those living in the cities, a big thank you for sharing favorite recipes and also for your kind patience while the cookbook was being completed. It d not have been possible without you.

CONTRIBUTORS

Adkins, Marilyn . . . . Sidney
Anderson, Dorrayne . . . . Kalispell
Annis, Connie . . . . Zurich
Arnt, Pat . . . . Augusta
Ausen, Ruth . . . . Bridger
Badt, Erma . . . . Hamilton
Baker, Jean . . . . Glasgow
Baker, Mrs. J.J. . . . . Lustre
Baldry, Dolores . . . . Billings
Baldry, Rodney . . . . Billings
Berge, Sally . . . . Billings
Berwick, Penny . . . . Bainville
Bischoff, Thelma . . . . Red Lodge
Black, Bessie . . . . Dodson
Black, Lorraine . . . . Belgrade
Black, Vera . . . . Dodson
Blow, Claudia . . . . Butte
Bramlette, Inez . . . . Fort Benton
Brookman, Vicky . . . . Billings
Callen, Betty . . . . Billings
Campbell, Delores . . . . Malta
Clague, Evelyn . . . . Bozeman
Clark, Jane . . . . Billings
Cobb, Cecile . . . . Augusta
Courtney, Ed . . . . Missoula
Dahl, Gerry . . . . Glasgow
Daniels, Lois . . . . Billings
Dingman, Linda . . . . Glasgow
Downs, Henrietta . . . . Joliet
Dyrdahl, Clarice . . . . Malta
Dyrdahl, Rose . . . . Loring
Elerick, Doris . . . . Great Falls
Ferrell, Maureen . . . . Havre
Fisher, Beverly . . . . Chinook
Flynn, Marge . . . . Billings
Germeraad, Donna . . . . Nye
Gilbertson, Joan . . . . Belgrade
Grove, Jean . . . . Billings
Hahn, Sharon . . . . Billings
Heiser, Nancy . . . . Absarokee
Henry, Dora . . . . Dodson
Hertzler, Alice . . . . Billings
Hicks, Ann . . . . Conrad
Hicks, Bob . . . . Malta
Holman, Nita . . . . Missoula
Inman, Nancy . . . . Chinook
Johnson, Ann . . . . Malta
Jolicoeur, Sonja . . . . Helena
Jones, Pat . . . . Billings
Kelly, Martha R. . . . . Glendive
Kluge, June . . . . Ronan
Knutson, Helen . . . . Rollins
Koke, Gert . . . . Malta
Lodge, Joyce . . . . Dillon
Martin, Judi . . . . Glasgow
McCann, Laura . . . . Harlem
Medvit, Marion . . . . Butte
Norheim, Sherry . . . . Lavina
Robinson, Linda . . . . . W. Yellowstone
Robinson, Mrs. Fred . . . . Malta
Rookhuizen, Barbara . . . . Billings
Root, Lynne . . . . Billings
Salonen, Gaylene . . . . Great Falls
Schultz, Donna . . . . Great Falls
Scott, Esther . . . . Noxon
Scott, June . . . . Plentywood
Scott, Shirley . . . . Florence
Serrette, Bill . . . . Absarokee
Serrette, Joy . . . . Absarokee
Sitton, Donna . . . . Billings
Sommerfeld, Ruth . . . . Bozeman
Sprinkle, Sadie . . . . Chinook
Steele, Shirley . . . . Billings
Stimpfle, Marco . . . . Billings
Stoner, Mabel . . . . Outlook
Stout, Irene . . . . Harlem
Swenson, Judy . . . . Billings
Tayne, Kitty . . . . Dillon
Totman, Ada . . . . Malta
Tracer, Madeline . . . . Butte
Ulm, Cleo . . . . Stevensville
Ulrich, Betty . . . . Malta
Unterbrink, Kathi . . . . Billings
Voight, Anne Lee . . . . Bridger
Waylander, Joy . . . . Livingston
Wayne, Bonnie . . . . Greenough
Weaver, Florence . . . . Billings
Whitfield, Wanda . . . . Fromberg
Willard, Mary Ann . . . . Augusta
Zinne, Karen . . . . Billings

ACKNOWLEDGEMENTS

For informative sources used in writing paragraphs about Montana:

A Traveler's Companion to Montana History, Carroll Van West
Billings Gazette Centennial Editions
Bitterroot Centennial Calendar, 1988-1989
Guide to Great Falls, Great Falls Tribune
It Happened in Montana, James A. Crutchfield
Montana, A History, Clark C. Spence
Montana: A History of Two Centuries, Michael Malone and Richard R. Roeder
Montana High, Wide, and Handsome, Joseph Kinsey Howard
Montana Our Land and People,
William A. Lang & Rex C. Myers
Names on the Face of Montana, Roberta Carkeek Cheney
The Montana Frontier, Merrill G. Burlingame

INDEX

APPETIZERS

BEVERAGES

SOUPS

SALADS

BREADS

SIDE DISHES

MAIN DISHES

MAIN DISHES (continued)

SWEET TREATS

SWEET TREATS (continued)

SWEET TREATS (continued)

ROUNDUP

Heart of The West Press
P.O. Box 80663
Billings, Montana 59102

Please send _______ copy(ies) of FAVORITE MONTANA RECIPES @ $15.95 each plus $2.00 postage.

NAME: ____

ADDRESS: ____

CITY: ____________________ STATE _________ ZIP __________

Enclosed is check or money order.

===

Heart of The West Press
P.O. Box 80663
Billings, Montana 59102

Please send _______ copy(ies) of FAVORITE MONTANA RECIPES @ $15.95 each plus $2.00 postage.

NAME: ____

ADDRESS: ____

CITY: ____________________ STATE _________ ZIP __________

Enclosed is check or money order.

===

Heart of The West Press
P.O. Box 80663
Billings, Montana 59102

Please send _______ copy(ies) of FAVORITE MONTANA RECIPES @ $15.95 each plus $2.00 postage.

NAME: ____

ADDRESS: ____

CITY: ____________________ STATE _________ ZIP __________

Enclosed is check or money order.

Heart of The West Press
P.O. Box 80663
Billings, Montana 59102

Please send _______ copy(ies) of FAVORITE MONTANA RECIPES @ $15.95 each plus $2.00 postage.

NAME:____

ADDRESS:____

CITY:_____________________STATE_________ZIP__________

Enclosed is check or money order.

==

Heart of The West Press
P.O. Box 80663
Billings, Montana 59102

Please send _______ copy(ies) of FAVORITE MONTANA RECIPES @ $15.95 each plus $2.00 postage.

NAME:____

ADDRESS:____

CITY:_____________________STATE_________ZIP__________

Enclosed is check or money order.

==

Heart of The West Press
P.O. Box 80663
Billings, Montana 59102

Please send _______ copy(ies) of FAVORITE MONTANA RECIPES @ $15.95 each plus $2.00 postage.

NAME:____

ADDRESS:____

CITY:_____________________STATE_________ZIP__________

Enclosed is check or money order.